HIKING & BIKING IN COOK COUNTY, ILLINOIS

HIKING & BIKING IN COOK COUNTY, ILLINOIS

by Jim Hochgesang

Design by Melanie Lawson
Editing and Nature Notes by Sheryl DeVore
Cover Photography by Hank Erdmann

A Roots & Wings Publication

Dedication

"There are but two lasting bequests we can give our children, one is roots, the other wings."

Hodding Carter

This book is dedicated to my Mom, Catherine Hochgesang, who always provided the roots and helped me develop my wings.

Created by Sandy and Jim Hochgesang
Offset printing service by Rheitone, Inc.
Printed and bound by United Graphics, Inc.

Roots & Wings assumes no responsibility or liability for accidents or injuries by people using this book to explore the hiking and bicycling trails described.

ISBN 1-884721-02-8

Printed on
recycled paper.

Contents

Acknowledgments

We appreciate the support, input, and guidance of many professionals who reviewed our draft manuscript, provided source maps, and supplied information.

Ders Anderson, Chicago Openlands Project
George Bellovics, Illinois Department of Natural Resources
Jim Louthen and John O'Lear, Forest Preserve District of
    Cook County
Jean and Paul Mooring, Illinois Prairie Path
Valerie Spale, Save the Prairie Society
Leanne Redden, Village of Schaumburg
Pat Moser, Palatine Park District
Deanna Shoss, Chicago Park District
Janet and Phil Whitfield, Chicago Botanic Garden
Paul D'Agostino, Evanston Park District
Bill Enright, Village of Arlington Heights
Bill Banks, City of Palos Heights
Lee Hanson, Illinois & Michigan Canal National Heritage
    Corridor
Jennifer Browning Skosey, North Park Village Nature Center

A special thanks to the women and men involved in developing and maintaining the trails and pathways in Cook and the adjoining counties.

Introduction

One early spring day while looking out a fast food restaurant window in downtown Chicago, it struck me that the only living organisms I saw were humans. These were stressed-out humans, walking hurriedly to get done whatever needed to be done as soon as possible. There was brick, concrete, plastic, metal, no trees, no shrubs, no flowers, no animals.

People like me often equate Chicago and Cook County with noisy, busy O'Hare International Airport and backed-up traffic with honking cars and nothing green to see for miles. But my exploring of the 310 miles of off-road trails and bike paths through forest and prairies along rivers and streams in Chicago and the surrounding suburbs of Cook County has shown me that this one-sided impression of one of the nation's busiest places is untrue.

You don't have to leave Chicago and travel far away to national parks, the mountains or the seashore, to find your peace and solitude. It's only a few minutes from O'Hare to a peaceful bicycle ride through the 14,000-acre Palos Forest Preserves. In fact, the Forest Preserve District of Cook County owns and manages over 67,000 acres of forests, wetlands, meadow, and prairies for you to explore. There are also many community parks in the county which offer havens from hectic lives. Also old railroad right-of-ways have been converted to trails. At these natural areas, we can take time to play and to recharge our batteries by walking, hiking, biking, running, cross-country skiing, in-line skating, and horseback riding.

This guidebook shows you how to find your slice of wilderness right here in Cook County. You'll find out about trails and paths in natural settings, how to get there, and the interesting flora and fauna you will find along the way. There's respite right here from work, school, social, and family obligations. Think of these sites as nature's health club and you as a charter member.

How to Use This Guide:

You will find a Cook County map identifying the trail locations on pages 20 and 21. Next, you will notice a summary table listing information such as trail length and type of surface for each site.

More detailed information on each site is provided in the individual sections. You'll learn how to get to the site, where to park, what facilities and amenities are available such as bicycle racks, restrooms, and drinking fountains, as well as special information about plants and animals living in or visiting the area. Other attractions such as nature centers will be described. Following the summary table, 22 sections describe trails and bike paths starting with the Des Plaines River Trail. It seems a fitting place to start since the first known exploration of the Chicago area by Europeans occurred here in 1673 when Louis Jolliet and Father Marquette searched for a connection from the Great Lakes to the Mississippi River. Throughout the county, trails and bike paths follow river greenways such as those along the Des Plaines. Forest preserves often were established along the rivers, creeks, and streams where the flood plains escaped development due to nature's propensity to produce spring rain and the resultant flooding.

Suburban Cook County, outside of Chicago's urban environment, cradles the city on the north, west, and south with Lake Michigan serving as the eastern border of the Chicago city limits. The next several sections will describe trails and bike paths in the northwestern part of the county followed by the southwest and southern areas. Here trails wander along or near Tinley Creek and Thorn Creek. The Chicago Park District Bikeway offers an off-road connection between the southern and northern suburbs along beautiful Lake Michigan with some gorgeous views of the city skyline.

Sections 19-22 describe trails and bike paths through or near the North Shore communities.

Following the narratives of the existing Cook County trails and bike paths, Section 23 describes the Greenway trail plans throughout Chicagoland and beyond including the Grand Illinois Trail which will extend 475 miles from the Chicago Portage site at Lyons in Cook County west to the Mississippi River, then north to Galena before looping back to Chicago. The target is to complete this massive trail system by the year 2000. You can hike and bike much of it today.

Hiking

What we describe as hiking in this guidebook can encompass leisure walking as well as a brisk run. All the trails described in this guidebook are open for hiking.

Several forest preserves have a two pathway system—a paved asphalt bike path as well as less-developed unpaved multi-use trails. Both types of trails are open for hiking. The multi-use trails might have a crushed limestone, packed earth, cinder, or woodchip surface. As well as being a peaceful place, the forest provides the hiker with oxygen given off by the trees and plants rather than the carbon monoxide and other pollutants generated on the streets and highways. Also, the bird songs are better than the traffic noise.

Cook County has trails to meet varying needs. Distances from less than 1 mile to 20 miles or more are available. A good place for a short hike with young children is at one of the five forest preserve nature centers.

Winter in the Botanic Garden.

Biking

This guidebook focuses on off-road trails and bike paths. You can bicycle 20, 50, 100, or more miles on interconnected trail systems such as the Illinois Prairie Path, Green Bay Trail, or North Branch Trail in Cook and the surrounding counties. This guidebook describes how you can get from one trail system to another nearby pathway. In some cases on-road bike routes are described for connection between two off-road trail systems. If you want to get the cyclist's perspective on the region's street system, the *Chicagoland Bicycle Map* is an excellent resource. Produced and sold by the Chicagoland Bicycle Federation (CBF), 312-42-PEDAL, the map recommends a regional network of on-street bike routes in addition to showing where the major off-road trails are. The City of Chicago and CBF also distribute the free *Chicago Bicycling Map*, which gives details for the Loop and the North Branch Trail and Lakefront Path connections in addition to showing the network of on-street bike routes in Chicago. Also the City of Chicago Bureau of Traffic (312-744-0645) offers a free booklet "Safe Bicycling in Chicago". This 32-page booklet describes what equipment you'll need, how to park and lock your bike, as well as important safety information that has specifics to Chicago but is very useful for bicycling any place particularly in an urban environment. Several suburban Cook County community park districts such as Palatine and Schaumburg offer bike path maps. (See the sections describing the community trails for more information.) Also you will find a listing of Cook County bicycle shops on pages 154-156.

Mountain Biking

Mountain biking has become a popular sport nationally. In Colorado, the gondolas and chair lifts used in the winter by skiers are now filled in the summer with people transporting their bikes up the mountain. While you won't find any mountains in Cook County to ride, there are many designated unpaved trails in the forest preserves open for mountain biking. Originally developed as bridal paths for equestrians, these trails are also used by hikers. You'll find tree roots, loose gravel, mud puddles, and washouts on these less used trails. Some are not suitable for road bikes. Most of these trails wind through scenic woodlands and along creeks and rivers. In this guidebook we describe which trails are more suitable for mountain or hybrid bicycles. Some forest preserve and nature center trails are closed for bicycling to protect the natural areas. Be sure to comply with the trail-use signs at the trailheads.

Cross-country skiing

When the snow falls, you will find that most of the trails and bike paths described in this book offer great places to cross-country ski. The Forest Preserve District of Cook County grooms trails in several preserves. The table on pages 22–25 lists trails open for cross-country skiing. Ski rental equipment is also available at several sites.

Forest Preserve District of Cook County Trail System

The Forest Preserve District of Cook County has five sites containing both paved asphalt bicycle trails and unpaved multi-use pathways, Deer Grove, Salt Creek, North Branch, Tinley Creek, and Thorn Creek. Some multi-use trails also serve as designated cross-country ski trails in winter.

The paved bicycle trails are open for hikers, runners, wheelchair users, and in-line skaters but not equestrians. Most forest preserve unpaved multi-use trails are open to all trail users except, of course, motorized vehicles. While the bike paths are all well-maintained and have signs that point the way for trail users, this is not currently the case for most of the multi-use trails. In some preserves, there are signposts in the parking areas containing a cross-country ski trail map, which identifies trail access. But the intersections on the trails have little to no signage so it's easy to get lost.

While the trail surface for the bicycle trails is a consistent asphalt surface (except for Arie Crown Preserve), the multi-use trails have a mixture of surfaces: crushed limestone, cinders, packed earth, mowed turf, and woodchip. The multi-use trails also have roots, tree stumps, washouts, mudholes, horse droppings, an occasional tree across the trail, and bumpy areas from equestrian traffic. Be careful. It's easy to get lost and you may not see another trail user for some distance. So why not stick to the asphalt bicycle trails?

Many trail users will probably want to do so. Others will want to venture onto the less developed trails to experience more variety, adventure, and less traffic. Bicyclists should have a mountain or hybrid bike to negotiate most of these trails effectively.

Nature Interpretive Facilities

A highlight of the Cook County Forest Preserves is the interpretive facilities provided at four nature centers, Camp Sagawau, and Trailside Museum. You will find excellent hiking trails at the nature centers and Camp Sagawau. As well as exhibits and displays, there are many programs about natural history, ecology, and wildlife. All these sites are described in some detail in this guidebook.

Rules of the Trail

The popularity of off-road trails continues to grow. As a result, you may encounter bicyclists, runners, wheelchair users, hikers, equestrians, and in-line skaters. Please be courteous and considerate of others so that everyone can enjoy our Cook County trails. Safety suggestions and regulations to protect the environment are described following this section. Please read them carefully. Also some sites have specific speed limits for bicycles. Check the signage on the trails for any site specific trail rules.

Nearby Attractions, Calendar of Events, Organizations

In the appendices, you will find a list of attractions and area merchants located in the Illinois and Michigan Canal National Heritage Corridor which begins in Cook County and runs southwest along the old Illinois & Michigan Canal to Peru in LaSalle County west of Starved Rock State Park. Also included is a listing of Cook County bike shops. A monthly calendar of events includes annual Cook County activities. You will also find a listing of environmental, hiking, bicycling, and other related organizations.

While we worked to find as many appropriate events and organization listings as we could, certainly some have been missed. Please notify us of any oversights for future issues of this guidebook. Our address is Roots & Wings, P. O. Box 167, Lake Forest, Illinois 60045.

Comments/Order Form

To improve future editions of *Hiking & Biking in Cook County, Illinois*, your comments would be very much appreciated. A form is on page 163. We'd also like to know if you'd be interested in future guidebooks. Page 164 contains an order form for those who want to purchase additional copies of this book or our first two publications *Hiking & Biking in Lake County, Illinois* and *Hiking & Biking in DuPage County, Illinois*.

Rules of the Trail

- Deposit litter in proper receptacles.
- Leave nature as you find it for others to enjoy. Remain on the trail.
- Leash all pets. (Some preserves do not allow pets.)
- Be alert for cars or bicycles.
- Don't feed the wildlife.
- Cook County Forest Preserves are open from sunrise to sunset daily. Hours of operation for most other sites are shown in the sections describing each site.
- Don't wear earphones. You can't hear a bicyclist coming.
- Relax, have fun, and enjoy!
- Check for ticks when you're finished.

Specific for Bicyclists
- Wear a helmet.
- Be alert for loose gravel, debris, holes, or bumps on the trails.
- Take it easy with hikers of all ages on the trail.
- Ride in single file.
- Cautiously pass hikers and equestrians on the left. Call out "passing on the left". But remember the hiker may be deaf or hard of hearing or may be wearing earphones.
- Keep both hands on your handle bars.
- Keep to designated bike trails in the forest preserves.
- See "Illinois Bicycle Rules" for additional safety information for on-road bicycling.

For your enjoyment
- Apply insect repellent before you go out depending on the season.
- Take water on long hikes or bike rides.

A Little History

Legend says that Chicago's name was derived from Checagou, an Algonquin word describing the aroma of the skunk cabbage and wild onions these Native Americans found growing along the river banks near Lake Michigan. For centuries, Native Americans used a 9-mile crossing to get from Lake Michigan to the Des Plaines River to pursue hunting, trading, and other endeavors.

Europeans and colonists discovered this crossing called the Chicago Portage in 1673 when a Franciscan priest, Father Marquette and explorer Louis Jolliet, were searching for a waterway connection between the Great Lakes and the Pacific Ocean. Traveling via canoe down the Fox River, they worked their way to the Mississippi and on down to Arkansas. Their exploration confirmed that the river continued to the Gulf of Mexico and not to the Pacific.

On their return north to Green Bay, Native Americans near present day Ottawa told them of a shortcut back to the Great Lakes via the Des Plaines River which they

Forest Preserve District of Cook County

Marquette and Jolliet monument at the Chicago Portage.

took. In late summer, 1673, they headed northeast on the Illinois and
Des Plaines Rivers to a swampy, mosquito-infested divide in what is
now the community of Lyons in southwestern Cook County. Their
Native American guides led them to a small stream, Portage Creek.
From there they carried their supplies and canoes one and one-half
miles through the wetlands.

Portage Creek led to Mud Lake and to the Chicago River which in
turn led them to Lake Michigan for their return to Green Bay. With
this discovery, French fur traders began using the route to expand
their enterprise south and west. Later the British and colonists used
the route to do business with the Spanish in the St. Louis area. However, conflict with nearby Native Americans inhibited any significant
development for over a century.

Historic records suggest that Chicago's first full-time non-Native
American was Jean Baptiste DuSable, a trader born in Santo Domingo,
Haiti. DuSable's mother was probably a black slave and his father was
French. After establishing his trading post in the late 1770s, DuSable
married a Potowatami woman and raised three children.

Following the Indian Wars of the 1790s, Native Americans ceded to the new U. S. Government, as part of the Greenville Treaty, 6 square miles where the Chicago River flowed into Lake Michigan. General Henry Dearborn ordered a series of forts built to protect the settlers who were starting to move into the Northwest Territory. In 1804, Fort Dearborn was completed on the south bank near the mouth of the Chicago River where it emptied into Lake Michigan.

Relations between the settlers and militia and the nearby Native Americans remained uneasy for years partially due to the British's constant agitation. The War of 1812 began when the British attacked an American fort at Mackinaw in Michigan. The Fort Dearborn garrison was subsequently ordered evacuated. During the evacuation, many of the settlers and militia were killed by warriors from several tribes in what came to be called the Fort Dearborn Massacre. After the war, settlers trickled back into the Chicago settlement. Construction of a new and stronger Fort Dearborn was completed in 1817.

Today, 45 percent of Illinois' population lives in Cook County. It was not always that way. In the early 19th century, settlers first inhabited areas along or near the Ohio River. In fact, some 50 counties had been established in Illinois by 1831 when Cook County, encompassing present day DuPage, Lake, McHenry, Kane, and Will Counties, was formed. As such Cook County was one of the least populated of the counties during that time. But that was soon to change due to the need for a transportation route from the East Coast to the rapidly developing Midwest states.

While the portage provided a water route to the Mississippi, it was an arduous one, sometimes taking three days with men pushing and carrying their gear and canoes through muddy leech-infested channels. To truly open up the area to the west, a much more efficient water highway was needed. An 1816 treaty with the Potowatami provided the land to build a canal. Following the opening of the Erie Canal in 1825, the Great Lakes started to attract more settlers. In the 1830s settlers began to populate the Chicago area.

Construction of the Illinois & Michigan (I & M) Canal started in 1836. Financial troubles for the young state of Illinois stopped the work for a few years. The canal was finally opened in 1848 and, as a result, the Chicago Portage became obsolete. The canal extended for 96 miles from the South Branch of the Chicago River to Peru, with 15 locks, dams, and aqueducts along the way. Mules on the towpath pulled the barges and boats loaded with flour, grain, cotton, finished goods, and passengers. The Midwest now had a navigable waterway for transport to the East Coast and to the south. The impact on Chicago was immediate. In the decade after the canal was open, Chicago's population grew by 600% and railroads were built. Chicago was well on its way to becoming the transportation hub of the Midwest and a major financial center, "the city that works". Recognizing that industrial and residential development was gobbling up open space in Chicago and the surrounding Cook County suburbs, community leaders began to set aside and protect the remaining natural areas in the early 20th century.

Daniel Burnham, the architect of the 1893 World's Columbia Exposition, developed the *Plan of Chicago* in 1909. The plan called for a series of interconnected forest preserves, parks, and boulevards and for protection and expansion of the lakefront. In 1915, the Forest Preserve District of Cook County was established, one of the country's first such organizations. Its mission continues to be to protect, preserve, and restore the natural environment of the woodlands, wetlands, and prairies set aside as open lands countywide. Today 11 percent of Cook County's total land mass, over 67,000 acres, is dedicated forest preserves. Even so this is less than half per capita of the dedicated open land in the five Chicagoland collar counties.

The Forest Preserve District carries out its mission by acquiring additional open land which will allow interconnected greenways of natural areas. These greenways can provide trails and pathways from one forest preserve to another. The district also plans to restore 54,000 acres, 80% of the forest preserve total lands, to the pristine condition that existed prior to European settlement. That is an extremely challenging objective—one that will take decades to accomplish. But it is the right objective for today and for future generations.

Now on to the trails.

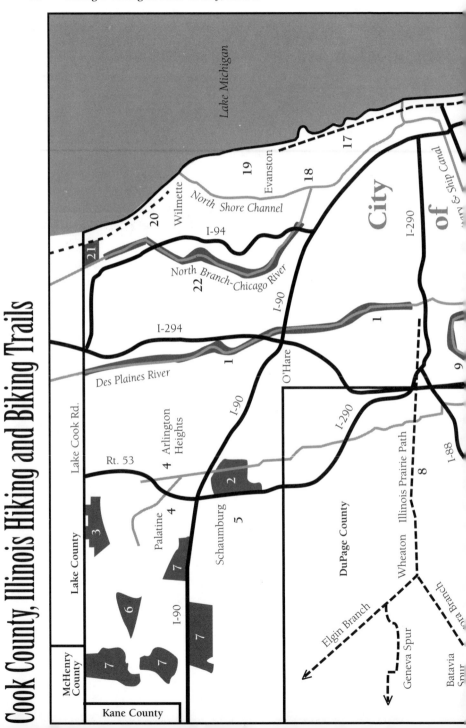

Cook County, Illinois Hiking and Biking Trails

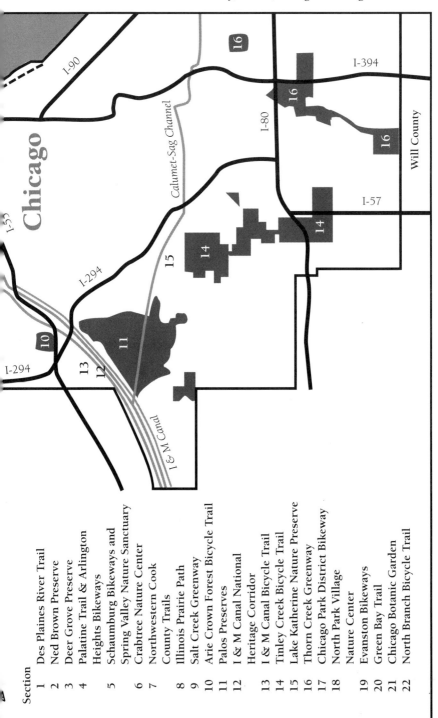

Section

1   Des Plaines River Trail
2   Ned Brown Preserve
3   Deer Grove Preserve
4   Palatine Trail & Arlington
    Heights Bikeways
5   Schaumburg Bikeways and
    Spring Valley Nature Sanctuary
6   Crabtree Nature Center
7   Northwestern Cook
    County Trails
8   Illinois Prairie Path
9   Salt Creek Greenway
10 Arie Crown Forest Bicycle Trail
11 Palos Preserves
12 I & M Canal National
    Heritage Corridor
13 I & M Canal Bicycle Trail
14 Tinley Creek Bicycle Trail
15 Lake Katherine Nature Preserve
16 Thorn Creek Greenway
17 Chicago Park District Bikeway
18 North Park Village
    Nature Center
19 Evanston Bikeways
20 Green Bay Trail
21 Chicago Botanic Garden
22 North Branch Bicycle Trail

Cook County, Illinois, Hiking and Biking Trails

Park, Preserve, or Trail	Section	Miles–Hike	/Bike	Surface	Author's Comments
Des Plaines River Trail	1				Trail will eventually run 60+ miles from Wisconsin border through Lake and Cook Counties.
Multi-use Trails		23.5*	23.5*	P	Good place for mountain biking. Open to equestrians. (See notes 1, 2 and 3.)
River Trail Nature Center		2.4	—	W	Hiking trails along the river.
Ottawa Trail/Chicago Portage		1	1	P	National Historic Site.
Ned Brown Preserve	2				A touch of nature next to Woodfield Mall.
Busse Woods Bicycle Trail		11.2	11.2	A	Popular spot for bicyclists, rollerbladers, runners and hikers.
Nature Trails		2	—	P, G	Footpaths through Busse Forest.
Deer Grove Preserve	3				One thousand acres of ravines, lakes, and forest.
Bicycle Trail		3.9	3.9	A	Recently part of the multi-use trail on the west side of the preserve was closed to bicycles. However a newly designated trail open to bicyclists and equestrians has been established.
Multi-use Trails		8.3	3.6	P	
Palatine Trail	4	6	6	A	Connects with Deer Grove Bicycle Trail. Also includes 5 miles of designated on-road bike route.
Arlington Heights Bikeways	4	5	5	A	McDonald Creek Bicycle Trail loops around Lake Arlington. On-road bike route connects to Busse Woods Bicycle Trail.
Schaumburg Bikeways	5	40*	40*	A	Connects to Busse Woods Bicycle Trail and Palatine Trail. Also includes 40 miles of designated on-road bike route.

Park, Preserve, or Trail	Section	Miles–Hike/Bike		Surface	Author's Comments
Spring Valley Nature Sanctuary	5	3.5	—	A, W	A 135-acre wildlife refuge with forest, prairie, and wetlands.
Crabtree Nature Center	6	3.3	—	W, P	Great bird watching and nature trails.
Northwestern Cook County Trails	7	*	*		Upcoming trail projects will interconnect Crabtree Nature Center with Paul Douglas, Poplar Creek, and Spring Lake Preserves in northwestern Cook County.
Beverly Lake		2.4	—	P	
Poplar Creek		4	3	P	1-mile hiking-only footpath through prairie. 3-mile multi-use trail. Open to equestrians.
Bode Lakes		1.5	1.5	M	
Illinois Prairie Path	8	55*	55*	L	First rails-to-trails conversion in the country. Main backbone trail system in DuPage County. Connects with many other trails. Four miles in Cook County to be upgraded in 1996. Open to equestrians.
Salt Creek Greenway	9	*	*		38-mile greenway trail planned.
Bemis Woods		5	5	P	Multi-use trail. Open to equestrians.
Salt Creek Bicycle Trail		6.6	6.6	A	Bicycle trail along the creek from Bemis Woods to Brookfield Zoo.
Wolf Road Prairie		2	—	C, M	88 acres of native prairie and oak savanna at this Illinois Nature Preserve.
Arie Crown Forest Bicycle Trail	10	3.2	3.2	P	Woodland trail through rolling terrain. Crushed limestone surface to be installed.

Park, Preserve, or Trail	Section	Miles–Hike/Bike		Surface	Author's Comments
Palos Preserves	11				14,000 acres of wilderness. Premier spot for hiking and biking.
Multi-use Trails		35	35	P; L	Open to equestrians.
Little Red Schoolhouse Nature Center		3	—	P; L	Nature exhibits and trails through oak forests. Hiking only.
Camp Sagawau		6.2	—	M	Only natural rock canyon in Cook County. Open for guided tours and cross-country skiing only.
Illinois & Michigan Canal National Heritage Corridor	12	20*	20*	L	Centennial Trail is planned for construction through Cook, DuPage and Will Counties. Will connect to 61-mile I & M Canal State Trail.
I & M Canal Bicycle Trail	13	8.9	8.9	A	Part of I & M Canal National Heritage Corridor. Good spot for beginning bicyclists: straight path with only one road crossing.
Tinley Creek Bicycle Trail	14	*	*		Two sections to be connected.
Northern Section		18.5	18.5	A	One of my favorites. Hilly trail through woodlands and meadows.
Southern Section		3.6	3.6	A	Loop trail is good place for beginning bicyclists. Flat terrain with no street crossings.
Lake Katherine Nature Preserve	15	3.3	—	W	Community of Palos Heights turned a 158-acre dumping ground into a beautiful natural habitat.
Thorn Creek Greenway Bicycle Trail	16	*	*		Two sections to be connected.
Northern Section		4.6	4.6	A	Trails along creek greenway.
Southern Section		4.7	4.7	A	Hilly pathway around Sauk Trail Lake.
Multi-use Trails		5	5	P	Good place for mountain biking and hiking. Open to equestrians.
Sand Ridge Nature Center		3.3	—	P	Once a sandy beach along Lake Chicago. Four hiking trails through woods and marsh.

Park, Preserve, or Trail	Section	Miles–Hike/Bike		Surface	Author's Comments
Chicago Park District Bikeway	17	18.5	18.5	A, C	Runs along Lake Michigan shore past beaches, parks, and museums.
North Park Village Nature Center	18	2.5	—	W	Forest, wetlands, and prairie in Chicago's only nature center. Hiking only.
Evanston Bikeways	19	8	8	A	Loops around Northwestern campus and along Lake Michigan and North Shore Channel.
Green Bay Trail	20	18	18	A, L	Old Indian trail connects with Lake County's North Shore Path which runs to Kenosha, Wisconsin.
Chicago Botanic Garden	21	7	—	A, L	Walk through prairie and woodlands as well as the magnificent gardens. Connects via sidewalk to Green Bay Trail. Trailhead for North Branch Bicycle Trail.
North Branch Trails	22				
Bicycle Trail		19.1	19.1	A	Popular bike path runs from Devon Avenue in Chicago to the Chicago Botanic Garden in Glencoe.
Multi-use Trail		8	8	P	Good place for mountain biking and hiking. Open to equestrians.
Nearby interconnecting trails	23				(See note 4).
North Shore Path		21*	21*	L	Lake County Trail connects via Green Bay Trail.
Fox River Trail		35	35	A	Kane County Trail connects via Illinois Prairie Path (IPP).
Prairie Trail-South		4.7*	4.7*	A	McHenry County Trail connects via IPP and Fox River Trail.

Note 1.) Surface designations: A- paved asphalt, L- crushed limestone, M- mowed turf, P-packed earth, W- woodchip. A mountain or hybrid bike is more effective on a mowed turf, packed earth, or woodchip trail.
Note 2.) Cross-country skiing in the winter is welcomed except for those trails designated hiking only.
Note 3.) *Signifies additional trails under construction or planned.
Note 4.) Other major trail systems in adjoining counties will interconnect with Cook County trails in the future. Some examples are Lake County's Des Plaines River Trail and DuPage County's portion of the 38-mile Salt Creek Greenway Trail. In Kane County, the Great Western Trail and the Virgil Gilman Trail will connect with the Fox River Trail which can be reached via the Illinois Prairie Path. In Will County, the Illinois & Michigan Canal State Trail and Centennial Trail will connect via the DuPage County portion of the Centennial Trail.

Des Plaines River Trail

The Des Plaines River begins in Wisconsin then flows through the Illinois counties of Lake, Cook, and Will before losing its identity in Grundy County where it merges with the Illinois River on its way to the Mississippi. The Des Plaines served as a major north/south transportation route for the Potowatami and other Native American tribes.

As settlers came to northeastern Illinois, communities developed along the river. Through several generations the waterway became a convenient sewer for residents and industry. During the last 25 years, pollution control efforts have helped to restore the Des Plaines. Thanks to the efforts of county agencies and communities along the way, water quality is much improved. Fish and waterfowl are more plentiful. With over 8,500 acres of Cook County forest preserves surrounding the river as it heads south, the river greenway offers open space and off-road trails amid the residential and commercial development.

Forest Preserve District of Cook County

Heron along the Des Plaines River.

Lake County

Today hikers and bicyclists can follow trails along the river through mature woodlands. In Lake County, there are two sections of improved multi-use trail open. The northern trailhead is in Van Patten Woods Forest Preserve near the Wisconsin border. Currently, this crushed gravel trail runs 9 miles south to Gurnee. The southern section starts near Libertyville and runs 8.8 miles along the river to Route 22 in Lincolnshire. There are several forest preserves along the way with pathways leading through mature woods, savanna, and wetlands. Farther south in Lake County there is a short unimproved trail from Lake Cook Road north into Ryerson Woods. A new pedestrian bridge over Lake Cook Road was constructed in 1995 as part of a road-widening project. Connecting existing Lake and Cook County Des Plaines River trails is a major step forward in completing a continuous greenway trail system. The Lake County Forest Preserve District has plans for trail additions over the next few years. Eventually a 33-mile trail will traverse the county along the river greenway. To learn more about the Lake County Des Plaines River Trail, see our

Lake County guidebook or contact the Lake County Forest Preserve District at 847-367-6640.

Cook County—Northern Section

Along the Des Plaines River in Cook County, you will find a series of forest preserves surrounding the river for its journey south. For many years, the Forest Preserve District has provided 23.5 miles of mostly continuous trails starting at Lake Cook Road and running south to Madison Street in River Forest. The 11-mile northern section runs from Lake Cook Road to Rand Road near Des Plaines. The southern (Indian Boundary) section consists of 12.5 miles of trail from Algonquin Road to Madison Street in River Forest. The pathways are primarily an unimproved packed-earth surface along or near the river mostly used by equestrians and hikers. On my visits, I've encountered few trail users except near the River Trail Nature Center described on page 30. Hikers and mountain bikers looking for seclusion and a bit of wilderness will enjoy this trail. Be aware that the path runs through the river bottom land and is sometimes impassable or muddy in spots, particularly after the spring showers.

How to get there:

You can park at several forest preserves along the way. The closest to the northern Cook County border is the Potowatami Woods Forest Preserve. Take Milwaukee Avenue (Route 21) south of Lake Cook Road 1 mile to Dundee Road. Turn left (east) on Dundee for .2 mile to the forest preserve entrance on the north side of Dundee. Park in the first lot. The unpaved, multi-use trail is to the west. (See map.) A bit farther east on Dundee, you'll find parking at the Dam No.1 Woods to the south. The trail intersects the auto road near the forest preserve entrance. Parking here avoids crossing very busy Dundee Road. The closest parking to the southern trailhead is near Morton Grove. Take Golf Road west of the Tri-State Tollway to East River Road. Turn south .1 mile to the Big Bend Lake Preserve entrance to the west. Trail access is near the entrance.

From the Lake County border at Lake Cook Road, the trail leads south through Potowatami Woods Preserve. The mature maple trees

Des Plaines River Trail/Northern Section

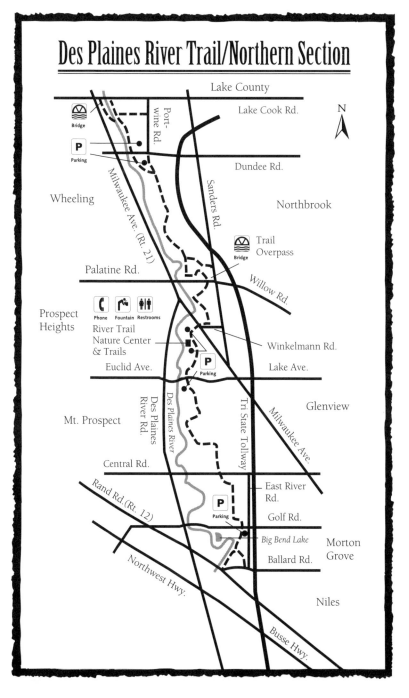

turn beautiful reds and yellows in fall. A side trail to the east (left) runs out to Portwine Road. A bridge across the Des Plaines offers another short side trail heading back north to Lake Cook Road. Caution! The road crossing at Dundee Road is extremely busy. South of Dundee is a 4-mile stretch with no street crossings due to a bridge over Palatine/Willow Road. The path ventures away from the river in this section. Watch out for washout areas here. One mile south of the overpass, the off-road trail ends at Winkleman Road. Head right on the street for .1 mile to cross very busy Milwaukee Road (Route 21). A stoplight is definitely needed here. I would not recommend crossing here or at Dundee with young children. The off-road trail picks up again in Allison Woods Preserve on the left side of the auto road heading south into the woods.

You'll soon come to the River Trail Nature Center. (See below.) The nature trails are for hiking only. If you're bicycling, you'll find a bike rack near the exhibit building. Continuing south there is another very busy street crossing at Euclid Avenue with high curbs so walk your bike. The trail continues south for 5 miles with two more road crossings at Central and Golf Roads before ending at Ballard and Rand Roads near Des Plaines. (See map.) Over the next few years the Forest Preserve District of Cook County plans to improve the existing multi-use trail. Hopefully, someday soon this entire stretch will be continuous with overpasses or stoplights at the busy road crossings as well as have an improved surface. For now, I would recommend this trail for hikers and mountain bikers looking for a bit of wilderness and isolation amid the surrounding communities. To avoid any road crossings, park in the Dam No. I Woods Preserve off Dundee as described above and head south to Winkleman Road then backtrack. From Dundee to Winkleman and back is an 8-mile round-trip with no road crossings. You will find rustic restrooms, water pumps, picnic tables, and shelters near the parking areas along the way. The trail is also open to cross-country skiers.

River Trail Nature Center

Nestled along the banks of the Des Plaines, the River Trail Nature Center has both indoor and outdoor animal exhibits, hiking trails, and historical displays ranging from the origins of our present day domestic apples to beehives to the Native American tribes who lived in this area hundreds of years ago.

How to get there:

The entrance is to the west on Milwaukee Avenue (Route 21) .7 mile south of the Route 45 intersection and north of Euclid Avenue. You can also bicycle or hike there on the Des Plaines River Trail. A bike rack is available at the nature center.

Hiking trails can be found north and south of the exhibit building. The Grove Portage Trail is a .5-mile loop through tall sugar maples. The trailhead is south of the exhibit building. Pick up a trail guide to learn more about sugar maples, the river floodplain, as well as the animals that live here. Benches along the way offer a secluded, tranquil spot to rest and listen to the birds. Note the sign at the trail intersection half way around the loop. The path to the east leads to the Des Plaines River multi-use trail.

Back at the nature center, you can see a red-tailed hawk, a falcon, great-horned and barred owls, and a fox at the outdoor exhibits. Inside are fish, snakes, and other animals. Here you can see the massasauga rattlesnake—Cook County's only venomous snake. Northeast of the nature center near the animal exhibits is the trailhead for the Little Fort and Green Bay Trails. Both are loop trails that lead to the Allison Woods Forest Preserve to the north. (See map.) Along the way, you'll cross over Agimak Creek, a stream that's usually dried up in the summer. Take the path to Allison Woods and note the work of beavers along the river bank north of the shelter. You will see three huge maple trees gnawed halfway through but left standing. On the path back to the nature center, the trail leads to the river. As I hiked here one spring afternoon, a sandhill crane flew low over the river heading south. Watching this large, graceful bird pass by through the trees, made me realize that the Des Plaines River serves as an effective greenway for many different animals even though it's sandwiched between highways, roads, and suburban neighborhoods. A round-trip of both nature center loop trails including the trail to Allison Woods is 1.9 miles.

Nature programs are offered year-round at River Trail. Call 847-824-8360 for more information. Restrooms, a drinking fountain, and public telephone are available at the nature center. Picnic tables and a shelter are available at Allison Woods. The nature center trails are also open for cross-country skiing in winter.

Southern Section
Indian Boundary Preserves

From Algonquin Road in Des Plaines to Madison Avenue in River Forest, an unpaved, multi-use trail runs 12.5 miles through the Indian Boundary Preserves. In 1816, the Potowatami deeded to the U. S. government a 20-mile wide strip of land which ran 80 miles from Lake Michigan in Chicago southwest to Ottawa. The settlers now had a route to establish a canal that would lead to the Mississippi River. The northern boundary line is a short distance south of Grand Avenue in Franklin Park.

How to get there:

From the north, take Algonquin Road west of the Tri-State Tollway. Turn south into the Campground Road Woods Preserve parking area .3 mile east of Des Plaines River Road. From the south take Thatcher Avenue north of Lake Street to Chicago Avenue. Head west to the Thatcher Woods Preserve entrance.

The Des Plaines River Trail picks up again at Algonquin Road heading south to River Forest. The trail runs through mature woodlands. But as in the section farther north, you'll find washouts, mudholes, loose gravel, and tree roots along the trail. A mountain or hybrid bicycle is much more effective here. Also unmarked side trails make it easy to get lost, often starting out 8-foot wide and narrowing to a 2-foot wide path in the river bottom land. The Forest Preserve District requests bicyclists and equestrians to stay on the main trail and avoid these narrow paths.

In Park Ridge east of and close to the Tri-State and O'Hare Airport, the trail is flat and smooth through a beautiful woods. Evans Field Preserve south of Fullterton was the site of a Potowatami village. Nearby were Native American burial grounds, prehistoric mounds,

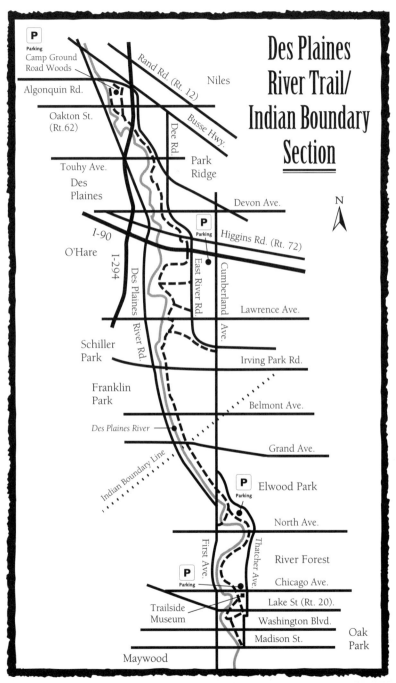

Des Plaines River Trail/ Indian Boundary Section

and other villages.

There are 14 road crossings from Algonquin to Madison Street, many across busy streets. In a few spots, the crossing is easy; for example you'll find an underpass at First Avenue and a fenced pathway on a bridge along Dee Road over the Kennedy Expressway. At Devon Avenue, there is an underpass, but I found it filled with mud and water making it fine for an equestrian or an adventurous mountain biker but not for a hiker or me on my road bike.

Hiking or biking the entire 12.5-mile multi-use trail through the Indian Boundary area would be tough today. I biked or hiked most of it in pieces. The Forest Preserve District plans to develop an improved multi-use trail the entire length and to connect it with the northern section described earlier.

Trailside Museum

Along the Des Plaines River Trail in River Forest is the Trailside Museum of Natural History. Through the years a finishing school, an orphanage, as well as a private residence have been housed here. Today the Forest Preserve District's wildlife rehabilitation center personnel care for injured and orphaned wild animals. When the animal's health is restored, it is released into the wild.

How to get there:

Take Chicago Avenue west of Harlem to Thatcher Avenue in River Forest. The museum is located in the southwest corner of the intersection. Parking is available on Chicago Avenue west of Thatcher.

The nature center has several animal exhibits inside and outside as well as natural history information. Programs are offered year-round. Call 708-366-6530 for more information.

Chicago Portage/Ottawa Trail Woods

If you want to see where Jolliet and Marquette discovered a connection between the Great Lakes and the Mississippi River, hike through the 300-acre Ottawa Trail Woods Preserve and Chicago Portage Woods in Lyons.

How to Get There:

Take Harlem Avenue south of Joliet Road. The first entrance to the west is for Ottawa Trail Woods Preserve parking area. A bit farther south on Harlem is the Chicago Portage Woods parking area.

At Chicago Portage Woods is a National Historic Site with a monument honoring Marquette and Jolliet. You can take the short footpath to Portage Creek to the south and another out to the Des Plaines River to the west. (See the history section for more about the Chicago Portage).

In Ottawa Trail Woods, you'll find a footpath along the river leading to Laughton's Ford. Two hundred years ago Indian trails radiated out from this focal point, one to Grosse Point (present day Wilmette) another southwest to Ottawa. An interpretive facility is planned at Laughton's Ford near the river. This center will include a museum, a library, a replica of the old Laughton's Trading Post, as well as an archaeological facility.

Future Trail Development and Interconnections

Today you'll find no trails along the river south of Madison Street to Ogden Avenue. But you'll discover a good place to hike nearby at Brookfield Zoo. The Salt Creek Bicycle Trail's eastern trailhead is at 31st Street just north of the zoo. (See Section 9.) Salt Creek and the Des Plaines River merge south of the zoo in Brookfield. There are plans to interconnect the Des Plaines River Trail and the Salt Creek Bicycle Trail over the next few years. Also the Des Plaines River Trail will be extended south along the river through forest preserves to the Chicago Portage National Historic Site. In the near future a 20-mile Centennial Trail will be constructed from the Portage Site south to Lockport along the Des Plaines River and the I & M Canal. The Centennial Trail will serve as a gateway to both the Grand Illinois Trail (see Section 23) and to the Illinois & Michigan Canal National Heritage Corridor (see Section 12).

Ned Brown Preserve

An 11.2-mile paved asphalt bicycle trail meanders through woods and around the 590-acre Busse Lake at the Ned Brown Preserve east of Schaumburg. Here you'll also find the 427-acre Busse Forest, a registered national landmark and nature preserve due to its rich variety of upland and lowland native tree species.

In warm weather, the preserve bustles with activity from the noticeable fishermen, boaters, bicyclers, and hikers, to the much less obvious wildlife. In fact, there are 2.5 million visits to this preserve each year—more than to Yellowstone National Park. But you still can find places for solitude in this huge 3,700-acre preserve.

The aquatic vegetation in the shallows and drop-off areas of the lake provide perfect habitat for northern pike, bullhead, crappie, and other fish. Many species of migrating ducks as well as shorebirds such as yellowlegs (named because of their long, bright yellow legs) seek the shallows to dine on succulent lake greens to fatten themselves up in

Forest Preserve District of Cook County

Island in Busse Lake at Ned Brown Preserve.

spring or fall before finishing their journey.

An invisible intricate food web occurs at Busse Lake. First, microscopic plant life are devoured by the microscopic daphnia shrimp which are then gobbled up by fry, or young fish. These, in turn, become a meal for a green-backed heron, which might then become dinner for hawk soaring overhead.

Filled with oak, basswood, and maple trees, the wooded areas provide cooling respite for hikers and bicyclists on a warm summer day. White oaks and basswood thrive in the dryer uplands while swamp white oaks and ashes grow well in the wetter lowlands. In spring, the woods burst with spring wildflowers such as great white trillium and wild geranium, catching the sun's rays before the trees leaves unfurl and block the light.

How to get there:

Ned Brown Preserve is bordered by Route 53 on the west, Golf Road and I-90 north, Arlington Heights Road east, and Biesterfield Road to the south. Higgins Road (Route 72) runs through the preserve. Parking is available near the bike path at the following locations: on Golf Road .2 mile east of Route 53, on Arlington Heights Road north of Higgins, and another location south of Landmeier Road. Parking is also available at four locations on Higgins between Arlington Heights Road and Route 53. On the south side take Biesterfield Road east to Bisner Road then north on Bisner to the entrance on the left. (See map.) If you're biking to the preserve, take the Schaumburg Bikeways east along Woodfield Road. From the Arlington Heights Bikeways, take the Wilke Road route south to Golf Road.

Busse Woods Bicycle Trail

While you can enter the bike path at many different locations along the way, we will describe a tour starting at Bisner Road on the south side. This decision was based on a thorough study of wind currents and traffic flow as well as where I parked on my first visit. The path runs north of and parallel to the Bisner Road entrance parking areas. The trail consists of a 7.8-mile loop plus several spurs out to communities along the way. Park in the first section available, and head right on the pathway. At the first trail intersection, turn left (north). The trail crosses over the south pool of the lake and runs by the Busse Lake boating center. Here you can rent a boat and will find a refreshment stand open in warm weather. The lake meanders through the preserve with small islands in several spots. The path continues north and crosses Higgins Road at a stoplight 1.9 miles out. Use the push-to-walk button. To cover the entire route turn left at the trail intersection north of Higgins. This path leads through the Ned Brown Meadow and near a model airplane field then turns east along Golf Road crossing over Salt Creek where it enters the preserve. Here the off-road trail ends near an I-90 underpass. An on-road Arlington Heights bike route starts at Wilke Road heading north.

To continue on the forest preserve bicycle trail, turn back and return to the trail intersection north of Higgins Road. Take the path to the left heading southeast along Higgins. At 7.6 miles out, the trail enters Busse Forest and heads northeast. Here the previously relatively flat terrain becomes a long gradual climb before turning south with a long descent. Don't be surprised if you round a curve and come face

Ned Brown Preserve

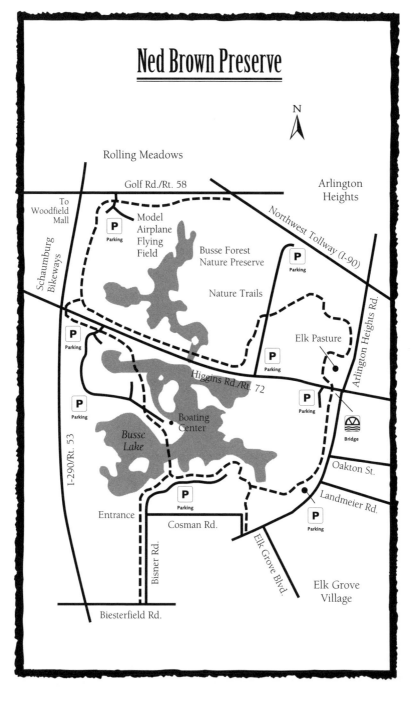

to face with a large elk with a full set of antlers. At 9.5 miles out, the path skirts around a fence enclosing a 14-acre pasture. Approximately a dozen elk reside here today. Two hundred years ago their ancestors roamed free in this area.

At 10 miles out, there is a safe crossing over busy Higgins Road on a new bridge opened in 1995. After a short distance through an open meadow, the path re-enters the woods for a bit heading south. Continue through the parking area as the trail turns back west. Stay on the path to the right to return to the Bisner Road parking area. From our starting point, the pathway continues south another .9 mile along Bisner to Biesterfield Road.

In warm weather, the Busse Woods Bicycle Path is one of the more heavily used trails in Cook County so relax and take it easy. You'll find water pumps, picnic tables, and restrooms at all the parking areas along the way.

A public telephone is available at the boating center. The paved asphalt path is in good shape, clean and well-maintained although you'll find some cracks along the way. In the winter, the bicycle path is open for cross-country skiing.

Nature Trails

A great place to hike is the Busse Forest nature trail in the northeastern part of the preserve.

How to get there:

From Higgins Road, take the eastern-most entrance road north 1 mile to the parking area on the east side of the road. The trail entrance is across the road north of an Illinois Nature Preserve sign.

The pathway meanders through an oak, sugar maple and basswood forest. Partially packed-earth and sometimes gravel surfaced, the 2 miles of narrow footpath meanders through the nature preserve. Here the voices of birds and insects drown out the traffic noise. There were very few hikers on my visits. If you are looking for a peaceful, quiet walk in a beautiful woods, you will enjoy Busse Forest. The nature trails are open to hiking only to protect the preserve.

Deer Grove Preserve

Filled with ravines, marshes, and lakes, Deer Grove Preserve is one of the best places to hike or bicycle in Cook County. A 3.9-mile paved asphalt bicycle trail and 8.3 miles of unpaved, multi-use trail wander through the woodlands and meadows of this 1,000-acre preserve.

How to get there:

Take Dundee Road west of Route 53 and Rand Road and east of Ela Road. There are three entrances off Dundee and one off Quentin Road which bisects the preserve. (See map.) If you use the asphalt bike trail, the best place to park is the eastern entrance on Dundee .5 mile west of Hicks Road. Direct access to the multi-use trail is available from the Quentin Road entrance as well as the middle (often closed) and western entrances off Dundee. On bike or foot, the Palatine Trail connects with the Deer Grove Bicycle Trail at the intersection of Dundee and Quentin Roads.

The asphalt bicycle path crosses the auto road near the first parking area of the easternmost entrance. Modern restrooms, a water pump, picnic tables, and shelters are available here. Heading east, the 10-foot wide bike trail runs through open fields and meadows with new growth trees nearby. After crossing over a creek, the trail turns north and loops back west along the creek. Larger trees grow here near the stream. At 2 miles out, a trail intersection offers two alternatives. The path left returns to the parking area completing the 2.8-mile loop. The path to the right leads to the central section of the preserve with a mature woodland, hills and deep ravines. (Note the map and trail rules at the intersection.) A ravine, a fragile ecosystem, hosts some unusual plant and animal life. Along the edges, for instance, you may notice the jewelweed growing, soft orange blooms in summer that attract hummingbirds. In the clear shallow water areas, look for tiny insects that seem to walk on water. These water striders grasp the tension of the water's surface to stay afloat and prey on tiny insects. Heading west, the path climbs as you enter an oak and maple forest. Camp Reinberg is to your left. The only road crossing is 2.5 miles out at Quentin Road. Be careful crossing this busy highway.

The bike path is to the left. An auto road to the right leads to several parking areas farther in the woods. About .4 mile west of the Quentin crossing, the bike path intersects with the auto road. Turn left and head up the hill on the auto road for .1 mile to pick up the continuation of the off-road bike path southeast of the parking area. The trail ends at the intersection of Quentin and Dundee Roads.

Note the inscription on the stone marker to the right of the trail. You'll find a message left from those who had the foresight to establish the Forest Preserve District of Cook County 80 years ago. While the language is a bit stilted and somewhat chauvinistic, the message will still carry forward to the 21st century.

"The Heritage to Posterity"

"The Forest Preserve District organized February 11, 1915 is the heritage of far seeing men of Cook County and Illinois, who by legislative act, seek to perpetuate the forest and streams, hills and vales, prairies and fields for another generation than this.... To the athletically inclined there are outdoor sports—to the fisherman well-stocked streams—to the

horticulturist the wildflowers—to the tourist comfort—to the infirmed hope—to the future the untrammeled, unmolested virgin fields and forests—our tribute to future generations..... Anton J. Cermak, President"

You can connect here with a 4.8-mile off-road segment of the Palatine Trail. (See Section 4.) Take the asphalt sidewalk on the southeastern corner of the intersection heading east for .2 mile and then south through the woods on the Palatine Trail. If you're not taking the Palatine Trail, you'll need to retrace your route back east.

Multi-use Trails

As well as the bicycle path, there are 8.3 miles of multi-use trail at Deer Grove through the forest and hilly terrain west of Quentin Road. These pathways range from 2-10 foot wide with a packed-earth or gravel surface. Serving as hiking, equestrian, and cross-country ski trails, these unpaved, multi-use trails are bumpy and narrow in spots due to loose gravel, roots, and horse tracks. The map on page 44 shows both trail systems. The multi-use trail is excellent for hiking since it is less used than the bike path.. It's a good place for a quiet

Forest Preserve District of Cook County

Cross-country skiers at Deer Grove.

Deer Grove Preserve

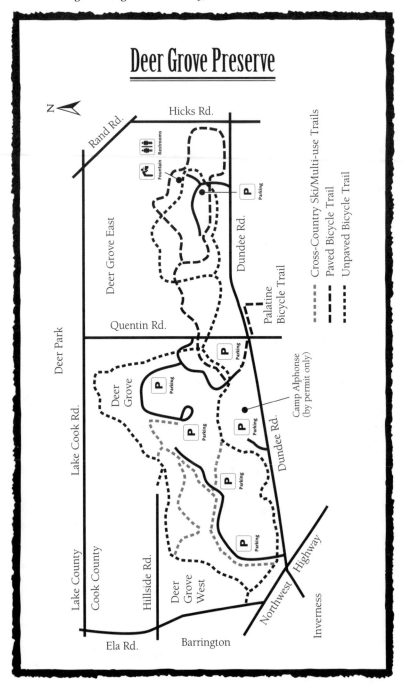

walk through the woods and along the lakes and marshes.

At the time of writing, part of the unpaved, multi-use trails on the west side of the preserve were closed to bicycling due to the damage to ground cover plants and the resulting erosion in the ravine area by off-trail bicycle use. As mountain biking has grown in popularity over the past few years, Deer Grove and the Palos Preserves have become favorite spots attracting many single track enthusiasts. However the hills and ravines of Deer Grove and Palos are beautiful natural areas cherished by environmentalists. In the past the Forest Preserve District has not had a policy restricting trail use. The controversy became heated in 1995 as the Forest Preserve District employees met with representatives of environmental organizations and trail user groups to hammer out a policy.

Good things are coming out of the controversy. Restoration work days co-sponsored by the Forest Preserve District, environmental organizations, and trail user groups including mountain bike advocates will help with the recovery of the damaged natural areas. A comprehensive trail system has been developed that considers the restoration and protection of the natural ecosystems as well as the recreational opportunities. A newly designated 3.6-mile trail has been established for bicycle use. Educational brochures, maps and signage will be developed to help guide trail users. Check trail signage to determine status as to which trials are open for bicyclists.

In the winter, experienced cross-country skiers will find the hills and curves on the Deer Grove trails challenging. Water pumps, picnic tables, and rest rooms are available at several picnic areas along the trail.

Palatine Trail and Arlington Heights Bikeways

Two adjoining communities in Northwestern Cook County offer bikeway systems with a combination of off-road paths and on-street bike routes.

Palatine Trail

The Palatine Park District has developed a multi-use pathway that connects to the Deer Grove Bicycle Trail, Harper College, and adjacent community bikeway systems. Consisting of approximately 6 miles of off-road asphalt path and 5 miles of bike route on designated side streets, the Palatine Trail also offers access to neighborhood parks and schools.

Trail users on the Deer Grove Bicycle Trail can extend their excursion 4.8 miles one-way (9.6 round-trip) on a portion of the Palatine Trail. From the Deer Grove Preserve bicycle trailhead at Quentin and Dundee Roads, cross over to the southeast corner. Watch out for the high curb. The Palatine Trail starts along the south side of Dundee. First heading east for .2 mile, the trail turns south and leads into a quiet, peaceful woods. The pathway is both curvy and hilly as it travels along small bluffs. Palatine Hills Golf Course is to the left. Soon you will pass through Ashwood Park. Here an on-street bike route heads south on Hawk Street leading to the community center, the train station, and the Margreth Reimer Reservoir. Follow the bike route signs.

To continue east on the off-road trail proceed through the underpass at busy Hicks Road. Follow the bike route signs as the trail leads through residential neighborhoods along the Com Ed right-of-way. You'll pass by Lake Louise and Doug Lindberg Park where the trail turns south heading to Maple Park at Anderson Drive. Heading east on the street, Anderson leads to an underpass at Route 53 and a connection to the Arlington Heights Bikeway at Wilke Road.

Farther south is a short off-road trail near the Margreth Reimer Reservoir. An asphalt path leads up a massive hill to a scenic view of the area. North of the reservoir is the 7-acre Palatine Prairie, a cornucopia of changing sounds and colors. In spring, the female meadowlarks return to build their well-concealed nests in the prairie grasses while the males perch in nearby trees singing their melancholy love songs. At the same time pink prairie phlox emerge among last year's dried grasses. The tall grasses are complemented by the buzzing of myriad insects, which are necessary for pollination. To protect this native ecosystem, only a narrow footpath is open on the prairie for hiking.

How to get there:

From Quentin Road north of Palatine Road, take Wood Street east to the parking area.

A third off-road section, located in the southern part of Palatine, runs by Harper College and connects to the Schaumburg Bikeways north of Algonquin Road. Take an on-road bike route heading south from the reservoir along Quentin Road. Follow the bike route signs through residential neighborhoods to Peregrine Park.

You can get a large detailed map of the entire Palatine Trail depicting both off-road trails and on-road routes by calling the Palatine Park District at 847-991-0333.

On the east side of Palatine along Route 53 is the Twin Lakes Recreational Area managed by the Salt Creek Rural Park District.

How to get there:

Take Palatine Road west of Route 53. Turn left at the first stoplight (Winston Drive/Marilyn Court). Turn left at the first street and follow the signs to Twin Lakes.

Here you'll find a golf course, driving range, boat rental, and 1.5 miles of asphalt path around the lakes. Call 847-934-6050 for more information.

Arlington Heights Bikeways

The Village of Arlington Heights has a bikeway system connecting parks, schools, shopping areas, municipal buildings, and neighboring community bikeways. While much of the bikeway is a designated on-road route, an interesting off-road portion is the 3-mile McDonald Creek Trail around Lake Arlington and along McDonald Creek.

How to get there:

Take Palatine Road east of Arlington Heights Road to Windsor Drive. Head north on Windsor .2 mile to the Lake Arlington parking area on the east side of Windsor.

A 3-mile asphalt-surfaced trail loops around Lake Arlington with short pathways connecting three nearby parks. Benches are available along the way. From a trail intersection on the north side of the lake, a short path leads through Wildwood Park. On the west side of Windsor, the trail continues through two more parks. Follow the path through the willow trees south to Palatine Road in Willow Park. Then take the sidewalk north of Crabtree Drive where the off-road trail heads west (left) along the creek through a nice residential area to Camelot Park. Note the stone retention walls that were built along the creek to prevent soil erosion. After crossing Brookwood Drive, the trail continues north following the creek for another .7 mile to Hintz Road. You'll need to retrace your route to return to Lake Arlington.

Built as a flood control project, the lake offers many recreational opportunities. Paddle boat and sailboat rental as well as a concession stand are available during warm weather. The path around the lake is a good place for youngsters learning to ride a bicycle and for novice rollerbladers. Restrooms, drinking water, bike racks, a public telephone, and picnic tables are available at or near the Lake Arlington boathouse.

A recent addition to the Arlington Heights Bikeways is a 1.3-mile off-road path at Nickol Knoll Park.

How to get there:

From Dundee Road, take the first street east of Route 53, Kennicott Avenue, north to the park entrance.

The very hilly trail loops around a golf course and a fire department training station. Because of the steep hills, the path is not open to rollerbladers.

The on-road bike route along Wilke Road on the south side of Arlington Heights leads to Ned Brown Forest Preserve and from there to the Schaumburg Bikeways system. North of the Palatine Road/ Kennicott Avenue intersection follow the green bike route signs to an underpass at Route 53. Follow Anderson Drive west to connect to the Palatine Trail at Maple Park. An Arlington Heights Bikeways map is available from the Department of Planning and Community Development. Call 847-577-5672.

Schaumburg Bikeways and Spring Valley Nature Sanctuary

When you hear the name Schaumburg, you may think of Woodfield Mall, rapid development, and traffic congestion. But look further and you'll find some pleasant, green areas to ride your bike and a peaceful nature sanctuary with 3.5 miles of hiking trails.

Schaumburg Bikeways

The Village of Schaumburg has developed an extensive bicycle path system for its residents and visitors. Those seeking exercise and a respite from traffic congestion will find an 80-mile bikeway with 40 miles of off-street bike path and 40 miles of on-road routes with designated one-way bike lanes.

A striped lane separates the cyclist from the auto traffic on the on-road routes. In addition to the 80-mile existing system, another 10 miles are proposed for construction by the year 2000. Bicyclists can ride from the Busse Woods Bicycle Trail (see Section 2) east of Schaumburg to the village's Spring Valley

Village of Schaumburg

Father and son on the bike path.

Nature Sanctuary, to the Prairie Center for the Arts, to Harper College, and yes, to Woodfield Mall.

The bikeways connect residential neighborhoods, parks, schools, the community library, churches, and shopping areas extending into all areas of Schaumburg. As well as the sites mentioned earlier, the Schaumburg Bikeways system also connects with the Palatine Trail, the Arlington Heights Bikeways, and will connect with a planned off-road bike path through Elk Grove Village as well as an Illinois Department of Transportation bike path heading northwest along Algonquin Road. The bikeways system is much too extensive for us to even try to display here. A very detailed (3 ft. by 2 1/2 ft.) map is available from the Village of Schaumburg Planning Department. (Call 847-894-0007 X258).

Spring Valley Nature Sanctuary

Ellsworth Meineke was one Schaumburg resident who recognized the need to preserve part of this rapidly developing suburb. Upon his recommendation, the Schaumburg Park District purchased land in

1982 to develop the Spring Valley Nature Sanctuary, 135 acres of woods, meadows and wetlands. Park district officials and volunteers went to work to restore prairies, by doing prescribed burns which kill the non-native species and allow the dormant native plants to come alive. The district has also reforested some parts of the preserve to encourage diversity. As a result, you can hear rose-breasted grosbeaks singing their melodious robin-like song in the woods during spring or hear the soft buzzy call of savannah sparrows perched on forbs in the prairie.

How to get there:

West of Route 53, take Meacham Road south to Schaumburg Road. Head west on Schaumburg to the Spring Valley Nature Sanctuary main entrance on the south (left) side of the road. On bicycle, take the Schaumburg Bikeways system. (The nature trails here are not open to bicycles, but there is a rack near the visitor's center).

The Vera Meineke Nature Observation Building south of the parking area doubles as a visitor center. Stop in and pick up a trail map and other pamphlets. A detailed interpretive brochure provides information about the natural habitats along the way. The 1.2-mile Illinois Habitat Trail takes you to a tallgrass prairie, a marsh, and woodlands. Other trails lead to an arboretum (.8 mile), the Volkening Heritage Farm (.7 mile) and Merkle Cabin (.6 mile). The farm is being restored to approximate an 1880's homestead like one operated by the Boeger family who lived and worked the land here a century ago.

The grounds are open from 8 a.m. to 8 p.m. April through October and 8 a.m. to 5 p.m. November through March. The visitor center is open 9 a.m. to 5 p.m. daily. Nature programs are offered throughout the year. Call 847-980-2100 for more information.

Crabtree Nature Center

On an early May morning at Crabtree Nature Center, palm warblers fly in and out of bluebells and trout lilies snatching insects while three double-crested cormorants sail to the marshes to dive for breakfast.

A short 30 years ago, this scene would not have existed at Crabtree Nature Center, a Forest Preserve District sanctuary near Barrington. Most of the 1,100-acre preserve was farmland, but now, regenerated forests, marshes, lakes, prairie, and secondary growth attract countless flora and fauna. Some 260 species of birds have been seen here. In spring and fall, migrating waterfowl carried by the winds from Central and South America find this preserve a welcome place to refuel before continuing their journey. Bird watchers often set up their spotting scopes at a large lake along a trail to get closer looks of ruddy ducks, northern shovelers, bufflehead, and other colorful migratory waterfowl.

The nature trails here offer hikers opportunities to see and hear red-eyed vireos and scarlet tanagers in the woodlands and meadowlarks and bobolinks among the native prairie grasses such as big blue stem and Indian grass.

Bur Edge Nature Trail.

How to get there:

Take Palatine Road east of Algonquin Road and 1 mile west of Barrington Road. The entrance is to the north at Strover Road.

The 1.3-mile Bur Edge Nature Trail starts behind the exhibit building. Pick up a trail guide at a wooden box near the trailhead. The woodchip path loops around Sulky and Bullrush Ponds, through woods, and past Crabtree Lake. The .3-mile Great Hollow Trail forms a short loop off the nature trail near the exhibit building.

On my first visit in late April, I saw a flock of great white egrets, which are endangered in Illinois. They nest in trees on secluded islands and travel, sometimes for miles, to fish for their young. The Crabtree Preserve provides a wonderful smorgasbord for these birds. My wife and son also saw another kind of heron here, a green-backed heron. You can often find it poised like a statue gazing at the water's edge waiting to snatch a meal. You can also enjoy spring wildflowers such a trillium and violet along the trail and watch copious swallows snatching bugs off the water's surface.

On the east side of the Bur Edge Nature Trail, a 1.7 mile path leads to the Phantom Prairie. An 8-foot wide woodchip path allows easy access through this quiet, less-frequented area. Listen for the rollicking

Crabtree Nature Center

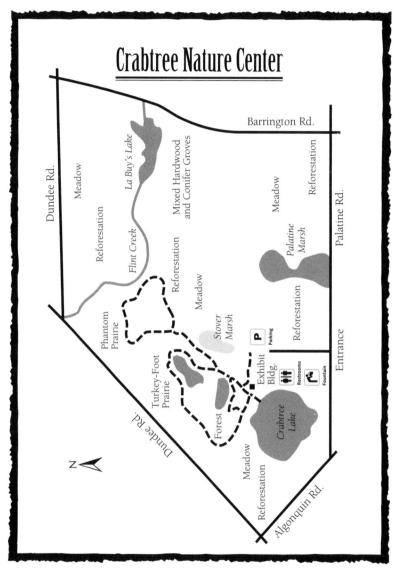

song of the bobolink, which looks like he's wearing a tuxedo with his
black back and white stomach. This rare songbird winters in Argentina.

A drinking fountain, phone, and restrooms are available at the
exhibit building. Nature programs are offered year-round including
bird walks. Call 847-381-6592.

Northwestern Cook County Trails

More than 7,300 acres of forest preserves await the hiker and biker in northwestern Cook County. Ned Brown, Deer Grove, and Crabtree Preserves have well-developed trail systems that are described elsewhere in this guidebook. Three other large sites will eventually be interconnected via the Algonquin Road bikeway currently under development and described in this section. Paul Douglas, Poplar Creek, and Spring Lake Preserves all have beautiful natural areas filled with oak forest, prairies, savannas, creeks, lakes, and ponds. Today there are some undeveloped trails that you may want to try.

Beverly Lake Trail

In the southern portion of Spring Lake Preserve, south of Barrington, is a popular fishing spot, Beverly Lake. There are 2.4 miles of designated cross-country ski trails west and north of the lake open to hiking year-round.

How to get there:

Take Higgins Road (Route 72) west of Sutton Road (Route 59) and east of Healy Road. The preserve entrance is to the north. The entrance road is bumpy, so go slow. Park to the left for trail access. The hilly trail winds along the lake and through an oak forest. There are loose rocks and roots on the rather rugged trail so watch your footing. Narrow footpaths lead off into the woods from the main pathway. Unfortunately the lake shore was littered with paper and pop cans on my visit. Some humans did not leave the preserve as they found it. There are no water pumps or restrooms here so bring water if it's a hot day.

Poplar Creek Preserve

Nature Conservancy volunteers and the Forest Preserve District of Cook County are restoring a 600-acre prairie and oak savanna here. The Shoe Factory Road Prairie in the northern section of the preserve was never farmed due to its rocky and hilly terrain. More than 100 species of forbs and grasses thrive here and rare birds like short-eared owls find this area a perfect hunting ground for field mice and other mammals that live in the prairie. Look in fall and spring for these large owls as they silently swoop like large moths to catch their prey. Bluebird boxes set up along the trails have attracted nesting bluebirds, a species whose numbers declined in the 1970s, but is now making a comeback due to man's intervention.

How to get there:

Take Golf Road (Route 58) west of Bartlett Road to Sutton Road (Route 59). Head north on Sutton to the Shoe Factory Woods Preserve entrance to the west. To see the prairie, park in the first parking area. Note the information signpost to the north. A brochure describing restoration efforts is usually available here.

Approximately 1 mile of narrow footpaths leads through the prairie. The tall prairie grasses such as Indian grass and big blue stem grow 6 or 7 foot high in the fall. *No bikes please!* There is also a 3-mile multi-use trail that loops around the preserve and runs past a large pond. Huge oak trees line the trail in some spots. The path crosses over Poplar Creek as it winds its way southwest to the Fox River.

Farther south, you can take a 1.5-mile hike around the Bode Lakes.

How to get there:

South of Golf Road, take Bode Road west of Barrington Road to the second Poplar Creek Preserve entrance on the right at Bode Lakes.

Follow the gravel and mowed grass trail around the two lakes. Poplar Creek runs east and west through the lakes. On a spring hike, a killdeer, a shorebird named because of its call, escorted me for a while stopping in the grass along the trail and then taking to flight as I approached.

You'll find water pumps, picnic tables, and rest rooms near the parking areas at Poplar Creek Preserve.

Algonquin Road Bikeway

Each beautiful forest preserve and natural area in northwestern Cook County is an island in terms of trail access (Crabtree Nature Center, Poplar Creek, Paul Douglas and Spring Lake Preserves). The only exception is Deer Grove Forest Preserve which can be directly accessed from the Palatine Trail. The rest must be reached by auto or by bicycling on often heavily traveled and congested highways. But that is about to change.

A major bikeway project, sponsored by the Forest Preserve District of Cook County, the Illinois Department of Transportation, and Hoffman Estates is under development. A trail will start at the southeastern section of Paul Douglas Preserve at the intersection of Roselle and Central in Hoffman Estates and wind its way 2.5 miles through the hills and wetlands of Paul Douglas Preserve. Meanwhile the Illinois Department of Transportation is constructing a 5.5-mile pathway along Algonquin Road from Roselle Road to Crabtree Preserve west of Barrington Road. The Forest Preserve District plans to construct a connecting trail from Algonquin to the Crabtree Nature Center.

Future plans call for extending this trail system east to connect with the Ned Brown Preserve and west to the Spring Lake and Poplar Creek Preserves. From there, extensions will lead to the 35-mile Fox River Bicycle Trail in Kane County, the 55-mile Illinois Prairie Path, and the proposed Tri-County State Park. When completed, trail users will have access to many wonderful natural areas via an extensive off-road trail network in northwestern Cook, Kane, and McHenry Counties.

The Illinois Prairie Path

Built on an abandoned railroad right-of-way, this 55-mile trail system runs as a single pathway west from the community of Maywood in Cook County across eastern DuPage County to the Illinois Prairie Path (IPP) focal point in Wheaton. From the Wheaton trailhead, a northwest branch leads to Elgin and a southwest trail runs to Aurora in Kane County. Spurs off the two west-bound branches run to Geneva on the northwest route and Batavia on the southwest. Shaped like a sideways rake, the IPP serves as the back-bone and connects with many other trails in the area. As a result, hikers and bikers have access to the most extensive inter-connected trail system in the Chicago area.

The IPP was built on the roadbed of the Chicago, Aurora, and Elgin Railroad (C.A.& E.), an electric line that served the western suburbs for 60 years from 1902 to 1961. A naturalist at The Morton Arbore-tum, May Theilgaard Watts, suggested turning the abandoned roadbed into a path system where people could walk and bicycle through natural areas. Watts, a teacher and an author of books and poems detailing the natural history of the Chicago area, was a well-respected environmentalist long before it was popular to be so.

Her visionary skills combined with the hard work of many other dedicated volunteers as well as local publicity helped carve the future for the IPP. The IPP became the first of many rails-to-trails conversions throughout the country and is recognized nationally.

In Cook and DuPage County, the trail is 10-foot wide crushed limestone. In Kane County, you will find asphalt as well as crushed limestone segments. The IPP is not a place to try to set a landspeed record. Some of the street crossings along the way are in quiet residential areas; others are in busy downtown areas. Please obey the stop signs. At most crossings, you'll find a metal post in the center of the trail as well as two posts near the sides of the path to keep out motorized vehicles. If you are biking, go slowly. Take your time and enjoy the parks, forest preserves, communities and other points of interest along the way. A map on page 62 displays the branches and spurs of the IPP as well as the major roads.

The DuPage and Kane sections, encompassing more than 50 miles of the IPP, are very well maintained and delightful places to hike or bike. That is currently not the case for part of the 4.5-mile Cook County section.

Main Stem (Eastern Branch)

The Main Stem section consists of 15 miles of trail from Maywood to downtown Wheaton in DuPage County. The Cook County trailhead is at busy First Avenue .3 mile north of I-290 in Maywood. Currently, there is no good parking convenient to the trailhead. Also, while the first mile of trail in Maywood is in good shape, the next 1.5 miles are not due to recent water main repair and lack of upkeep. Furthermore from Mannheim Road to 50th Avenue in Bellwood there is an on-road detour. The Illinois Department of Natural Resources plans to improve the Cook County section with construction slated for the second half of 1996. The Forest Preserve District of Cook County plans to extend the path .5 mile east across the Des Plaines River to the Chicago Transit Authority station at Des Plaines Avenue in Forest Park. In the interim, I would recommend skipping the first 3.5 miles of trail and starting farther west at Wolf Road in Hillside.

The Illinois Prairie Path

Running on the Illinois Prairie Path.

How to get there:

In Cook County, take Wolf Road south of St. Charles Road and .3 mile north of Butterfield Road (Route 56) to Eisenhower Park in Hillside. Park near the tennis courts at the back of the parking area. Access to the IPP is south of the courts.

Head west on the bridge over Wolf Road to the community of Berkeley. A park with picnic tables, drinking water, restrooms, and a bike rack is west of the bridge. The IPP runs under I-294 entering DuPage County at Elmhurst.

In Elmhurst, the community park district has restored 6 acres of tallgrass prairie from Salt Creek to Spring Road along the IPP. At the Berkley Street intersection, you will discover an interpretive garden labeling the native prairie plants our ancestors discovered hundreds of years ago.

Farther west are bridge crossings at Salt Creek and Route 83. At 3.2 miles out, the IPP enters Villa Park. Here you will pass the Villa Park Historical Society Museum and IPP Visitors Center at Villa Avenue. At 4.5 miles out, you will enter the community of Lombard. Mature trees

The Illinois Prairie Path

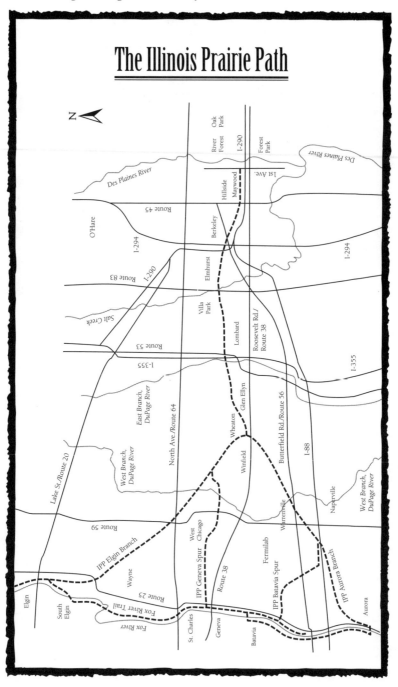

along the trail provide welcome shade in the warm weather. At 6.9 miles out leaving Lombard, you will pass a huge bridge over I-355 built for IPP users as well as a second bridge over the East Branch at the DuPage River.

In downtown Glen Ellyn after 8.6 miles is Prairie Path Park with benches, a water fountain, and a bike rack. The trail continues west into downtown Wheaton to the trailhead at Volunteer Park.

How to get there:

Outside of Cook County the best place to park is at the Wheaton trailhead. Take Route 53 or I-355 from the north or south. From I-355, exit Roosevelt Road west for 3.3 miles to Carlton Avenue. Head north on Carlton for .3 mile to the IPP trailhead in Volunteer Park at the intersection of Carlton and Liberty Drive.

You can park at the parking garage to the right for just $1 daily during the week. Weekends are free. You will also find metered parking the first block south on Carlton. Farther south is FREE four-hour parking on Carlton north of Roosevelt.

You will find a display case with information about the IPP as well as a free map and a water fountain at Volunteer Park. The name of the starting point is appropriate given the literally thousands of volunteers who have contributed their time and talents to make the IPP a premier trail system.

Elgin Branch

From the Wheaton trailhead at Liberty Drive and Carlton Avenue, take the pathway heading north over Volunteer Bridge. In 1983, volunteers restored the 160-foot-long iron truss bridge and added three 70-foot spans to cross over two city streets, a small park, and the railroad tracks. This portion of the IPP runs 15.7 miles to Elgin where it connects with the Fox River Trail. At .7 mile out is a good spot to observe the Lincoln Marsh Natural Area. An observation platform to your left has benches as well as stairs down to a platform by the water's edge. You will see Canada geese and other migrating waterfowl such as bufflehead ducks and mallards in spring and fall stopping to rest before heading to their wintering or breeding grounds. With a long straight stretch of trail, this is a very picturesque place. A short distance farther northwest, a wooden boardwalk leads to a woodchip nature trail through the marsh. This trail is for hikers only. Bicyclists can lock up at the bottom of the boardwalk.

At the County Farm/Geneva Road intersection (2.5 miles out), the IPP splits in two. The Geneva Spur, when completed in 1996, will head west along the south side of Geneva Road. The Elgin Branch continues in the northwest quadrant of the intersection. Here the IPP enters the Timber Ridge Forest Preserve. A new .8-mile multi-use trail also planned for completion in 1996 will head north through Timber Ridge on the west side of County Farm Road to Kline Creek Farm and the Great Western Trail. At 5 miles is a slough where beavers have done their work. On my visits here in 1995, cyclists had to port their bikes up a 20-foot climb to an intersection with the 12-mile Great Western Trail. Across the trail was a somewhat hidden path down the hill to continue heading northwest on the Elgin Branch. An improved crossing is scheduled for completion in 1996.

Farther west a North Avenue underpass simplifies the crossing of this very busy road. At Route 59 (approximately 6.4 miles out), a new pedestrian bridge was opened in fall, 1994. At 8.7 miles, there is a steep downhill grade to a railroad track crossing. There are roots and stumps on the narrow trail. Walk your bike through this area. A portable toilet and bench are at the Army Trail Road crossing at 9.1 miles. The entrance to Pratt's Wayne Woods Forest Preserve is .7 mile to the right on the Powis Road crossing at 9.2 miles out.

Back on the IPP, the path leads through marshes along the border of the forest preserve and then crosses over Norton Creek at 9.8 miles. Here the path enters into Pratt's Wayne Woods. The trail leads first through forest, then wetlands. Brewster Creek forms a pond in the marsh to the east. A bench along the trail is a good resting spot where you can enjoy a scenic view of the marsh. Leaving the forest preserve, the trail enters Kane County at 11 miles out at Dunham Road. Bridges provide a safe crossing over the Chicago Central and Pacific (C.C.P.) railroad tracks and Route 25.

Proceeding farther into Kane County, the woods give way to farmland. At 14 miles out, the path intersects with the Fox River Trail south of Elgin. The Fox River Trail heads south to Aurora and north to the McHenry County Prairie Trail which runs to Crystal Lake. The round-trip distance back to the Wheaton trailhead is 28 miles from this point. The IPP and the Fox River Trail coexist on the same pathway consisting of both off-road trail and on-street routes for another 1.7 miles heading north to Prairie Street in Elgin. The northern IPP trailhead is at Prairie Street north of the riverboat. Follow the bike path signs through Elgin if you want to continue north on the Fox River Trail.

Geneva Spur

The newest member of the IPP family of trail branches and spurs is the path to Geneva. In 1996, the DuPage County Division of Transportation will open 3.7 miles of crushed limestone trail from the southwest corner of the intersection of County Farm Road and Geneva Road in Winfield to Reed-Keppler Park in West Chicago. The trail will run through Winfield Mounds Forest Preserve with a bridge crossing over the West Branch of the DuPage River. At Reed-Keppler Park, 6.7 miles out from the Wheaton trailhead, the new path connects with the existing trail that leads to the Fox River Trail in Geneva.

West of Reed-Keppler Park, the IPP crosses over seven railroad tracks leading to the Metra maintenance station just outside West Chicago. Thanks to a very long bridge built for the trail users, it's an easy crossing. The path here is through mostly open prairie and marshland. Approximately 7 miles out, there are four very narrow (and easy to miss) pathways on the south side of the IPP that lead into the West Chicago Prairie Forest Preserve. The prairie trails are open to hikers only.

Farther west the IPP runs between the DuPage County Airport to the north and the Prairie Landing public golf course to the south. You'll find no trees here to provide shade nor any water fountains between Reed-Keppler Park and the Fox River in Geneva. Cornfields surround the path west of the golf course as it enters Kane County. There are only five street crossings over the 5 miles from West Chicago to Geneva. Unfortunately one at Kirk Road has extremely heavy traffic and high curbs. Be very careful here. I would not recommend crossing with young children. A bridge or a stoplight is definitely needed. At East Side Drive, the trail runs north (right) on a wide sidewalk to High Street. Head west on High Street for a short distance. The off-road path resumes to the right and enters Good Templar Park. The pathway crosses over a steep ravine on a bridge and proceeds to a switch-back ramp down to Route 25. Cross Route 25 cautiously. Across the road, the Geneva Spur meets the Fox River Trail. The Geneva Spur spans 8.6 miles from Winfield to Geneva.

Aurora Branch

From the northern trailhead at Volunteer Park in Wheaton, take the limestone path along Carlton Avenue .3 mile south to Roosevelt Road. The off-road trail begins south of Roosevelt Road.

At 1.5 miles out be careful crossing Orchard Road, a busy street where cars come fast around a curve in the road. At 2.5 miles out, there is a crossing at Wiesbrook Road. The IPP continues straight ahead across the street. The sidewalk on the west side of Wiesbrook Road in front of Wheaton-Warrenville South High School heads south .5 mile to the intersection with Butterfield Road. Diagonally across the street is a trail entrance to Herrick Lake Forest Preserve.

Continuing southwest on the IPP from Wiesbrook Road, the trail is tree-lined and peaceful. Three and one-half miles out is Saint James Farm, a large horse farm. A tunnel crosses under Butterfield Road at 3.7 miles out. The surrounding countryside is now mostly farmland as the path parallels Butterfield Road/Route 56 for a bit. At 4.1 miles, the IPP crosses Winfield Road at a stoplight. The IPP heads south along Winfield Road for about 300 feet and then west through Warrenville Grove Forest Preserve. This is a peaceful woodsy area. A bridge crosses over the West Branch of the DuPage River. As you enter Warrenville, the sidewalk on the west side of Batavia Road is the beginning of the bike path which heads north into Fermilab. Here you'll find a 4-mile bicycle path and 3.5 miles of hiking only nature trails through woods and prairie.

At 6.3 miles, there is a single lane tunnel under Route 59. Walk your bike through the underpass. The Batavia Spur heads off to the right at 7.3 miles out. (See next page.)

The Aurora Branch continues south with an underpass beneath I-88. At 8.2 miles, you will need to carry your bike over the Elgin, Joliet, and Eastern (E.J.& E.) railroad tracks. Power lines run along the trail for about 1.5 miles. Farther west, Eola Road and Farnsworth Road crossings are quite busy. Eola Road is being widened to four lanes. This project will include a bridge for the Aurora Branch and an underpass for the Batavia Spur. At 11 miles, you will cross over Indian Creek. The trail is tree-lined for a bit before entering the outskirts of Aurora. At 12.5 miles, follow the bike path sign onto Hankes Road. A very busy Route 25 crossing is at 12.6 miles. A stoplight is definitely needed here. Use caution when crossing. The IPP continues across the road and down a hill into a community park. The IPP parking area and southwestern trailhead is 13 miles out just north of Illinois Avenue and east of the Fox River. The IPP and the Fox River Trail are contiguous from Illinois Avenue to New York Street where you will find a riverwalk and another riverboat casino. If you are interested in continuing north on the Fox River Trail, cross over the river on Illinois Avenue to McCollough Park on the west bank. The Fox River southern trailhead is located there.

Batavia Spur

There are practically no trees here, mostly a lot of farm land. If you need a break, there's a bench where you can sit and listen to the corn grow. Soon you will come to another railroad track crossing. Two miles from the start of the spur, the pathway is again tree-lined and passes by two ponds. At 9.8 miles, the path enters Kane County. White and pink honeysuckles and wildflowers border the trail. At 11.2 miles out from the Wheaton trailhead, the path crosses very busy Kirk Road just west of Fermilab. I finally got across after a long wait. I don't recommend crossing with small children. The good news is that an overpass will be installed in 1996. This is a good example of the ongoing improvements on the IPP. If you take the asphalt path on the west side of Kirk Road heading north for .8 mile, you can access the Fermilab bike path at Pine Street.

West of Fermilab, the Kane County trail is asphalt-surfaced and tree-lined. After crossing Raddant and Hart Roads, you will come to the intersection with the Fox River Trail at 13.5 miles out from the start in Wheaton. One mile farther south on the Fox River Trail is the Red Oak Nature Center. The Batavia Spur continues north for another 1.1 miles contiguous with the Fox River Trail. The western trailhead is at the foot of the stairs leading up to Wilson Street in downtown Batavia.

The Cook County section is maintained by the Illinois Department of Natural Resources. The DuPage County portion of the IPP is maintained by the DuPage County Division of Transportation. For further information, call 708*-682-7318. In Kane County, the Kane County Forest Preserve District maintains the spurs and the Elgin Branch. The telephone number is 708*-232-5980. The Aurora Branch is maintained by the Fox Valley Park District (708*-897-0516).

If you are interested in becoming a member of the Illinois Prairie Path organization, you can obtain a membership application by writing to The Illinois Prairie Path, P. O. Box 1086, Wheaton, IL 60189 or calling 708*-752-0120. Members receive a quarterly newsletter and a large IPP map. Your contribution will help maintain and improve the IPP.

* Note DuPage County and the southern half of Kane County's area code changes to 630 in August 1996.

Salt Creek Greenway

Salt Creek runs through northwestern Cook County then flows south to DuPage County before heading back east into central Cook County where it empties into the Des Plaines River south of Brookfield. Much of the way forest preserve greenways surround the stream. While you'll find no salt water here today, there is a story that the name Salt Creek came from a 19th century farmer's mishap. His wagon, loaded with salt barrels, got stuck in the water during a crossing. The next day he discovered the salt had washed into the creek, thus his misadventure lives on. By the 1970s, with all the development in the western suburbs, water quality had deteriorated badly. Thanks to more effective sewage treatment and the establishment of natural area greenways surrounding the creek, water quality is much improved today. As a result, waterfowl and other wildlife have returned. You'll find trails at three sites along the Salt Creek greenway in central Cook County.

Susan Van Horn

Hank Erdmann

Spring in Bemis Woods.

Bemis Woods

A 5-mile unpaved, multi-use trail runs through the gently rolling terrain along or near Salt Creek in the Bemis Woods Preserve north of Western Springs. The western trailhead for the Salt Creek Bicycle Trail is also here.

How to get there:

Take Ogden Avenue (Route 34) .5 mile east of the Tri-State Tollway (I-294). The entrance is to the north. A second entrance is a bit far-

ther east off of Wolf Road .6 mile north of Ogden. Both entrances
have easy access to the multi-use trail. (See map.) The bicycle path
trailhead is only accessible from the Ogden Avenue entrance as described below.

The multi-use trail loops through hilly woodlands and along a
meandering creek. The surface is packed earth or loose gravel in some
spots. The pathway is mostly 8- to10-foot wide but narrows to a
single track overgrown with vegetation in some spots. It's easy to lose
your way with all the trail intersections, so bring a compass and map.
This trail is open to hikers, equestrians, and bicyclists. It offers a bit
more rugged alternative to the nearby asphalt trail. A mountain or
hybrid bike will more effectively handle the roots, stumps, and
washouts on the dirt pathways.

Salt Creek Bicycle Trail

The 6.6-mile paved asphalt path runs from Bemis Woods to Brookfield Zoo passing through or near the communities of Western
Springs, La Grange, La Grange Park, North Riverside, Westchester,
and finally Brookfield.

How to get there:

The western trailhead is in Bemis Woods Preserve off Ogden
Avenue as described above. Trail access is south of the toboggan slide.
The eastern trailhead is at Brookfield Woods Preserve northwest of
Brookfield Zoo. Take 31st Street west of Des Plaines Avenue and east
of La Grange Road (Route 45/12/20). Parking is also available in the
Brezina Woods Preserve off Mannheim Road. (See map.)

On an early May ride, wildflowers carpeted the woods along the
path. The trail is curvy and has some hills. There are five road crossings and several forest preserves along the way. Narrow side trails
head off along the creek and into the woods. Hugging the creek in
spots sometimes along small bluffs, the trail runs mostly through mature woodlands. A prairie restoration is underway north of the zoo.

Be particularly cautious at the five street crossings! You'll encounter
extremely heavy traffic at several crossings, especially, La Grange
Road. High curbs and no stoplights at some streets contribute to your

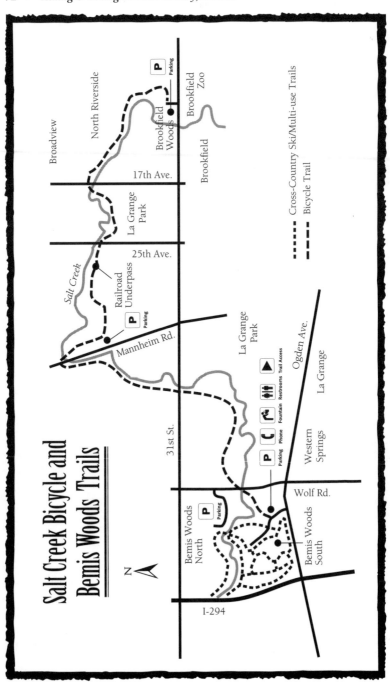

Salt Creek Bicycle and Bemis Woods Trails

N

Broadview

North Riverside

La Grange Park

Salt Creek

Railroad Underpass

Mannheim Rd.

17th Ave.

25th Ave.

Brookfield Woods

Brookfield Zoo

Brookfield

Parking

La Grange Park

Ogden Ave.

La Grange

31st St.

Western Springs

Wolf Rd.

Bemis Woods North

Bemis Woods South

I-294

Parking Phone Fountain Restrooms Trail Access

Cross-Country Ski/Multi-use Trails

Bicycle Trail

need for attention. Also there is a very steep downhill heading west at the Wolf Road crossing. A caution sign is needed here. Go slowly! I really enjoy this trail, but would not recommend bringing young children just learning to ride because of the road crossings. Bridges or stoplights with a push-to-walk button would really be helpful at the Wolf Road, 31st Street, and 17th Avenue crossings.

There are water pumps as well as rustic and modern restrooms, picnic tables, and shelters in the forest preserve picnic areas along the way. However, I couldn't find a water pump at the eastern trailhead in Brookfield Woods.

If you haven't encountered enough wildlife on the trail, head east on 31st Street .2 mile from the eastern trailhead at Brookfield Woods to tropical rain forests and African grasslands. The Forest Preserve District of Cook County owns and the Chicago Zoological Society operates the world famous Brookfield Zoo. Here you can observe more than 2,500 animals of 400 different species and enjoy a relaxing walk. Call 708-485-0263 for hours and admission prices.

In the near future, a 38-mile Salt Creek Greenway trail will run from the Ned Brown Forest Preserve in Cook County south through DuPage County's forest preserves and then east with an underpass at I-294 to Bemis Woods and the existing Salt Creek Bicycle Trail. The trail will pass through 13 communities from Elk Grove Village to North Riverside and interconnect 180 miles of trails and bike paths. At the time of writing, engineering work was underway and construction was expected to start in the spring of 1997. The target completion is 1998 depending on sufficient funding.

Wolf Road Prairie

Eighty-eight acres of oak savanna, prairie, and marsh thrive in this Illinois Nature Preserve in Westchester. The Depression helped to save the land, which had been planned for residential development in the 1920s, in its natural state. Also the wetlands here made the area ill-suited for growing crops or grazing animals. As a result, at Wolf Road Prairie, you can walk through land that is much like the first settlers encountered 160 years ago. Recognized as the finest and largest silt loam soil prairie east of the Mississippi, Wolf Road Prairie

Wolf Road Prairie in summer.

is incredibly diverse consisting of prairie, savanna, and wetlands. Some 400 plant species flourish here.

How to get there:

Take Ogden Avenue east of I-294 past Bemis Woods Forest Preserve to Wolf Road. Head north on Wolf Road to 31st Street. Head west (left) on 31st Street for .1 mile. There are three small concrete parking area pull-ins north of 31st Street. Park in the middle one. Here you can pick up an excellent trail guide at the information signpost.

The pathway near the entrance is a set of rectangular grids of concrete connected with narrow earthen footpaths. The concrete walkways are old sidewalks installed in the 1920s for the proposed residential development that never happened. Take the path to the right of the information signpost where you'll find a 250 year-old bur oak tree. This specimen is a perfect example of its species which, thanks to a thick, resilient bark survived the frequent fires that swept through and rejuvenated the prairie.

Smaller brethren surround the giant tree in an oak savanna, perhaps the rarest ecosystem in the world. Growing beneath the trademark bur oak in this combination forest/grassland are plants such as white rue anemones and wild hyacinths. In fall, the lovely woodland sunflower brightens the shady oaks with its yellow-hued petals.

The prairie blooms May through October. The trail guide describes what you will encounter such as muskrat, blue-winged teals, and other animals.

Valerie Spale and Phil Cihlar, volunteers in the Save the Prairie Society, gave me a tour of the prairie one hot day in late July. Having left my burnt-out lawn at home, I was struck by the vibrancy, color, and diversity that abounds in the summer heat. They pointed out prairie dock, yellow coneflowers, rattlesnake master, Indian grass, and myriad other forbs. Every few weeks different plants bloom and predominate. Ongoing burns and removal of alien plants keep the prairie thriving.

If you walk all the concrete sidewalks and hike out to the prairie house at the far northern section of the preserve, you will have a 2-mile hike. The prairie house has an interesting history and future. The German settlers in a small community called Franzosenbusch erected a two-room schoolhouse in 1852. Plans are to restore the original structure with a new role as a nature center. Once again, it will be a schoolhouse.

To protect the prairie plants, the path is open to hikers only. You can lock your bike at the signpost. Be sure to wear long pants. In summer and early fall, the trails can be overrun with the prairie plants. Also many of the concrete slabs have cracks and become uneven, so watch your step.

You'll find no facilities here so bring water on hot days. Several fast food restaurants are east of Wolf Road along 31st Street. The Wolf Road Prairie is preserved by a consortium consisting of an active volunteer group called Save the Prairie Society, the Illinois Department of Natural Resources, the Forest Preserve District of Cook County, and the Illinois Nature Preserves Commission.

Call 708-865-8736 for more information.

Arie Crown Forest Bicycle Trail

South of Countryside, you'll find a 3.2-mile woodland trail through rolling terrain.

How to get there:

Take the Stevenson Expressway (I-55) to La Grange Road. Head north. There are two preserve entrances to your left. The first is .3 mile north of the Stevenson. An auto road loops through the preserve with trail access in several locations. Signposts near the parking areas identify the trail access points. Another entrance is also on La Grange north of 67th Street near Lake Ida. A third entrance is off Joliet Road (Route 66) west of La Grange Road. Take Brainard Road south into the preserve.

Most forest preserve-designated bicycle trails in Cook County have a paved asphalt surface. This trail is unpaved. Mostly packed earth, the trail is bumpy and narrow in spots. I did ride the trail uneventfully on my road bike. The Forest Preserve District plans to install a crushed limestone surface. Until then, the trail is more suitable for mountain bikers. With several loops and trail intersections and no signage on the trail, it is easy

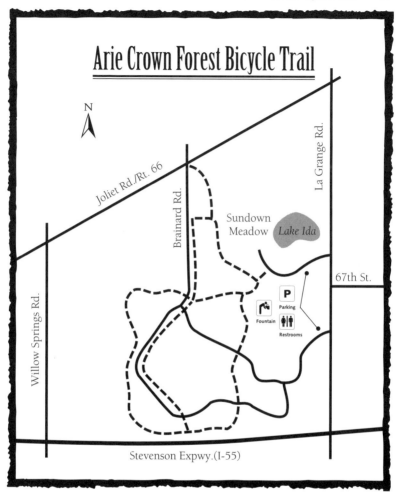

Arie Crown Forest Bicycle Trail

N

Joliet Rd./Rt. 66

Brainard Rd.

Sundown Meadow *Lake Ida*

La Grange Rd.

67th St.

P
Parking

Fountain

Restrooms

Willow Springs Rd.

Stevenson Expwy.(I-55)

to get lost so bring a map and a compass. Since the auto road crosses the trail in several spots, you won't be lost long. There are a few hills to climb, a small creek to cross over, and nearby Lake Ida. The northern portion is quiet and peaceful. Traffic sounds increase as you approach I-55 to the south.

The cross-county ski trail displayed on information signposts throughout the preserve is also the bicycle trail, unlike several other preserves where there are separate trails. Rustic restrooms, water pumps, and picnic tables are available near several of the parking areas.

Palos Preserves

Nestled in southwestern Cook County is perhaps the country's largest forest preserve site and definitely Chicagoland's largest. Visitors will discover lakes, ponds, forest, meadows, and sloughs throughout the 14,000-acre Palos Preserves. This is as close to wilderness as you can get in Chicagoland.

These preserves were formed by the last glacier that sculpted hills, canyons, and ravines leaving behind huge potholes from the melting ice to form lakes, ponds, and sloughs. Natural and man-made waterways border as well as intersect the preserves. The Des Plaines River, the Sanitary and Ship Canal, and the Illinois & Michigan Canal flow from the north part of the preserve southwest to the Illinois River. The Calumet-Sag Channel bisects the preserve and flows west to merge with the Sanitary and Ship Canal near the Du-Page/Cook County border.

You'll discover 35 miles of unpaved, multi-use trails through the Palos Preserves as well as many miles of addi-

tional footpaths branching from the main trail. You could hike at
Palos for a week and not cover every trail. The narrow footpaths are
not open for biking or horseback riding. You'll also find 3 miles of
hiking-only trails at the Little Red Schoolhouse Nature Center and 6.2
miles of trails for cross-country skiers and hikers at Camp Sagawau.

The boundless variety of ecosystems, flora, and fauna as well as the
many places for solitary journeys and challenging hills make the Palos
Preserves one of the best places for hiking and off-road bicycling in
Chicagoland. And if you want to learn your trees, the Palos Preserves
is where to do it! Sycamores and ironwood abound at McClaughry
Springs. Pawpaw trees and shingle oaks can be found in PawPaw
Woods. This is as far north as these native trees can survive. The
woods of Palos are filled with towering white oaks, the state tree, as
well as black and red oaks.

How to get there:

Given the enormous size and scope of the Palos Preserves, parking
locations are innumerable. We will describe recommended places to
park that provide easy trail access to the nature centers and the multi-
use trails. (See map.) North of the Cal-Sag Channel, from the Willow
Springs Road intersection with Archer Avenue (south of the Des
Plaines River), take Willow Springs south of 95th Street. Here Willow
Springs becomes 104th Avenue. Proceed south. The Little Red
Schoolhouse Nature Center entrance is on the west side. You can
access the multi-use trail south of the parking lot where it intersects
with the nature center path leading to the White Oak Trail.

Little Red School House Nature Center

A century ago, Palos Hills farmers sent their children to school in a
one-room log cabin near what is now the busy intersection of 95th
Street and La Grange Road. Classes continued until 1948. Seven years
later the Forest Preserve District converted the building to a nature
center. Inside children of all ages can explore the world of nature up-
close. In one area, busy bees perform intricate dances, spinning in
circles, moving forward and back. These dances give exact directions
to where other bees can find flowers producing nectar they need to

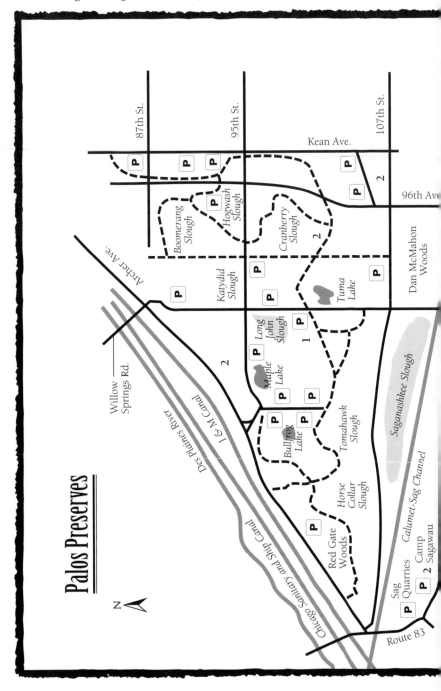

Palos Preserves

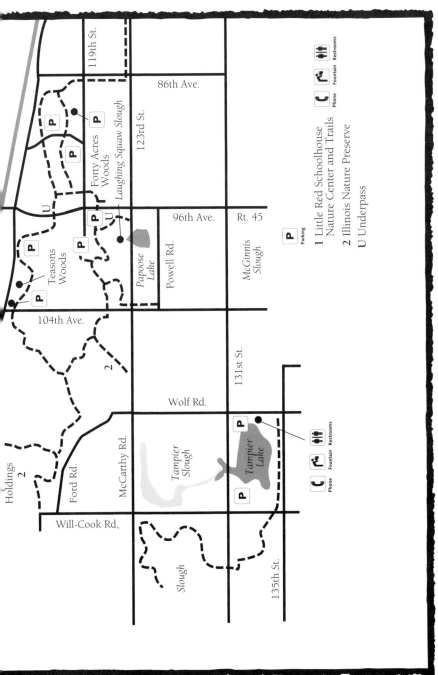

119th St.

86th Ave.

123rd St.

Laughing Squaw Slough

Forty Acres Woods

96th Ave.

Rt. 45

P P

P

P U

Powell Rd.

Papoose Lake

McGinnis Slough

P

P

Teasons Woods

P

104th Ave.

131st St.

2

Wolf Rd.

McCarthy Rd.

Tampier Slough

Tampier Lake

P

P

Holdings 2

Ford Rd.

Will-Cook Rd,

Slough

135th St.

Phone Fountain Restrooms

1 Little Red Schoolhouse
  Nature Center and Trails
2 Illinois Nature Preserve
  U Underpass

P
Parking

Phone Fountain Restrooms

make their honey. If you prefer snakes and snapping turtles, you can get close views of them inside the center as well.

Outside, more exhibits await you including a collection of 1880 vintage farm implements and interpretive signs providing a wealth of information on plants, animals, and ecosystems you will discover along the trails. One sign described mileage to nearby sites and those much farther away. For example, Lake Michigan is 16 miles from the preserve and the sun is 93 billion miles away. Luckily, the nature trails are a shorter distance. The .3-mile Farm Pond trail heads west from the center's rear leading to the 1.8-mile Black Oak trail. As you walk, look for the black oak's fallen acorns which have ragged-edged cups. Then look for a tree with deeply furrowed bark, toothed leaf lobes, and gray hairy buds. These native Illinois trees are rare, so enjoy them while you are here.

The Black Oak Trail winds on packed earth through wooded and hilly terrain and along the Long John Slough. In summer, you can enjoy the white flowers of the water lilies, a native species, covering much of the water's surface. In fall and spring, look for large numbers of waterfowl and shorebirds congregated on the slough. Near the shallow edges, you will find the dabbling ducks, such as a mallard that feeds by tipping up its body to reach down to snack on aquatic plants and seeds. In the deeper areas, look for diving ducks such as scaup that plunge into the water's depth, sometimes 20 feet, to snatch aquatic insects, plants and mollusks. You can identify a scaup by its blue bill with a dark point at the end, dark head and breast, golden-colored eye, and whitish body, with black rear.

South of the parking area you'll find the trailhead for the 1-mile White Oak Trail looping through white oaks. These trees have round-lobed leaves (as opposed to the black oak with its toothed leaves). The bark is only shallowly furrowed and gray, compared with the black oak's much darker bark. These hiking-only trails are a perfect place to take young children or for adults who want a short walk in the woods.

A water pump, bike rack, public phone, soda machine, and portable restrooms are available near the exhibit building. Nature walks and other programs are offered year-round. Call 708-839-6897.

Palos Multi-Use Trails/North of the Cal-Sag Channel

South of Archer Avenue and north of the Cal-Sag Channel is an 18-mile network of unpaved, multi-use trails with surfaces varying from packed earth to crushed limestone to cinder to gravel. The Forest Preserve District plans to install a crushed-limestone surface on all the multi-use trails here.

As you travel away from roads deeper into the forest, street noises fade into natural sounds. Chipmunks' piercing calls echo in the woods. Birds, especially in spring and early summer, sing as they flit from tree to tree. During spring migration, you'll enjoy a feast for the eyes. To stoke up for their long journey north to breed, colorful birds from the neotropics search for insects hiding in the trees' leaves. Bring your binoculars in May to enjoy some 30 kinds of warblers, tiny insect eaters with colorful patterns such as blue wings and yellow heads or black and red tails. Some will remain here to nest; others will fly farther north to Canada. Birds are attracted to water in spring and you may, for instance, discover a scarlet tanager with its deep red body and jet black wings, bathing in a creek on a warm spring day.

The terrain is hilly and climbs are challenging. You will be rewarded with lovely views of creeks, woods, lakes, ponds, and sloughs. Daniel Webster describes a slough as "an abyss. . . a place of deep mud or mire." At the Palos Preserves, the sloughs are more aptly defined as lakes and ponds brimming with wildlife. Their names are captivating and picturesque: Saganashkee, Crawdad, Red Wing, and Belly Deep.

The multi-use trails are open for hiking, bicycling, and horse riding. Be careful; you'll encounter many hilly areas with washouts as well as roots and rocks on the trail. The pathways are not well-marked, and you'll find many trail intersections, so bring a compass to avoid getting lost. You will eventually come out to a road or preserve picnic area where you can get your bearings. Water pumps, shelters, and rustic restrooms are located in most preserve picnic areas near the trails.

For bicyclists, a mountain or hybrid bike is recommended to handle these trails effectively. Please stay on the 8-foot wide maintained trails and don't venture off the path where you might disturb the fragile ecosystem. The narrow foot paths are not open to equestrians or bicyclists.

Forest Preserve District of Cook County

Toboggan slide at Swallow Cliff Woods.

Cross-country skiers will find 6.8 miles of trail open in winter near the Maple Lake area.

Sag Valley Multi-Use Trails
South of the Cal-Sag Channel, you will find 17 miles of unpaved, multi-use trail meandering through the hilly mature woodland areas.

How to get there:
Take Route 83 south to the Swallow Cliff Toboggan Slide entrance .2 mile west of 96th Avenue (Route 45).

Named for the bank swallows that nested in the cliffs here, the Swallow Cliff Woods is a good place to start your trek through the secluded wilderness.

Recently, controversy has arisen regarding the impact of mountain biking on the natural areas at Palos and Deer Grove Preserves. Both areas have rugged, hilly terrain that attract a growing number of mountain bikers. Unfortunately, some overzealous bicyclists have significantly damaged the vegetation in some sensitive natural areas, particularly the ravines. Consequently, at the time of writing, the narrow trails in the Swallow Cliff Woods area, south of the Cal-Sag Channel have been closed to bicycling while restoration of the ravines and other areas is underway. The Forest Preserve District plans to add signage that will help trail users know which trails are open to what type of use. Some 5 miles of crushed limestone surfaced trails remain open for bicyclists. Partnering with trail user groups and environmental organizations, the Forest Preserve District intends to protect the sensitive natural areas of Palos while offering challenging trails that recognize the popularity of mountain biking.

When the snow falls, cross-country skiers will find 6.2 miles of groomed trails here. You can also rent toboggans and take a break in the warming shelter as well as use the heated restrooms.

Camp Sagawau

On the far west side of the Palos Preserves south of the Cal-Sag Channel you will find Camp Sagawau, open by reservation only. Here you can hike through Cook County's only natural rock canyon.

Forest Preserve District of Cook County

Rock Canyon at Camp Sagawau.

Special programs include a canyon hike in which participants wade through a creek to enjoy the ferns, wildflowers, and rock formations. In spring, lush green ferns begin to unfold from closed fiddle-like branches to lacy green delights. Naturalists will also lead you on fossil hunts and in the winter, you can participate in Nordic ski clinics. The camp is open for cross-country skiing when the snow base is sufficient. For more information on how to take a trip through this unique area call 630-257-2045 (708 area code until August 1996).

How to get there:

Take Route 83 south of the Cal-Sag Channel and east of Archer Avenue. Route 83 is also 111th Street here. Proceed east for a short distance to the Camp Sagawau entrance on the north side of Route 83.

Tampier Lake Multi-Use Trail

You'll find another 4.5 miles of unpaved, multi-use trails south of McCarthy Road and west of Wolf Road near Tampier Lake and Tampier Slough.

How to get there:

Take Will-Cook Road south of McCarthy Road and 131st Street to the Tampier Lake entrance .1 mile south of 131st Street on the east side.

This multi-use trail is open for bicycling but is more suitable for mountain bikers as well as hikers. The .9-mile section south of Tampier Lake along 135th Street is relatively flat, bumpy, and not very interesting except for a nice view of the lake. The trail crosses Will-Cook Road and heads northwest through a large open field on a service road. North of 131st Street the trail becomes more interesting as it meanders through woods and open meadow before it dead ends at a slough. You can also rent rowboats at the boating center to get a different perspective of the lake.

The Palos Preserves provide trail users many unique adventures year-round. For the nature lover, there is no other place in Chicagoland that quite equals these preserves. So, enjoy and help protect these areas for future generations.

Illinois & Michigan Canal National Heritage Corridor

In 1984, Congress established the nation's first National Heritage Corridor to preserve the historic sites and natural areas along the 96-mile route of the Illinois & Michigan (I & M) Canal. (See pages 18–19 for a brief history of the canal.) Running from the Chicago River, which in the 19th Century flowed into Lake Michigan in downtown Chicago, to Peru in LaSalle County, the once grand 60-to-120-foot wide canal has shrunk to a narrow and shallow remnant of its former self due to erosion and natural filling of sedimentation.

As well as helping to preserve the buildings, locks, and other relics of the historic canal, the corridor serves as a first-rate greenway for hiking and biking trails. Describing all the sites, trails, and items of interest involved in the Heritage Corridor is beyond the scope of this guide-book. Our purpose here is to make Cook County trail users aware of some of the available recreational opportunities. Several of the Cook County trails and bike paths described in other sections of this book are part of the Heritage Corridor: I & M Canal Bicycle Trail, Arie Crown Forest Bicycle Trail, Salt Creek Bicycle Trail, Wolf Road Prairie, trails in the Palos Preserves and the Lake Katherine Nature Preserve.

A new Cook County trail, under development at the time of writing, will become a major gateway for Chicagoland trail users to visit and enjoy the many attractions and points of interest along the historic corridor. The Centennial Trail, when completed, will run through the Illinois & Michigan Canal National Heritage Corridor for 20 miles from the Chicago Portage site at Lyons in Cook County to Lockport in Will County. The10-foot wide trail bordered with 2-foot wide hiking and running paths will also be a key link in the 475-mile Grand Illinois Trail targeted for completion in the year 2000. (See Section 23.) Construction of the Centennial Trail is planned in Cook, DuPage, and Will Counties.

How to get there:

The northern trailhead will be located at the Chicago Portage National Historic Site in Lyons. Take Harlem Avenue south of Ogden Avenue to 47th Street in Lyons. The entrance is to the west.

From the portage site, the Centennial Trail will run on the north side of the Des Plaines River heading south to Willow Springs Road. After a bridge crossing over the river, the trail continues southwest between the river and the Chicago Sanitary & Ship Canal (near the existing Cook County I & M Canal Bicycle Trail described in Section 13). After passing by the Palos Preserves to the south, the Centennial Trail will enter DuPage County near the Waterfall Glen Forest Preserve which contains an excellent 9.5-mile loop trail around Argonne National Laboratory. After a 2.5-mile stretch through DuPage, the trail briefly re-enters the southwest corner of Cook County north of Lemont.

In Will County, a 3-mile section is open from the Cook/Will County border to just north of 135th Street in Romeoville near the Isle a la Cache Museum. The plan is to extend the trail south to 2nd Street in Lockport where it will connect with the existing 2.3-mile Gaylord Donnelley Canal Trail through downtown Lockport. Here you will find the I & M Canal Museum, a pioneer settlement, as well as the 1838 Gaylord Building containing the I & M Canal Visitor Center, the Illinois State Museum Gallery, and a restaurant. A few miles farther west lies 51.7 miles of I & M Canal State Trail that runs from Channahon to LaSalle along the canal tow path passing near the canyons of Starved Rock and Matthiessen State Parks. With the completion of the Centennial Trail and a section southwest of Lockport through Joliet, Chicagoland trail users will have easy access to a wonderful 100-mile corridor of off-road trails and pathways filled with history, natural greenways, and recreational opportunities.

We have included a summary of Heritage Corridor attractions, points of interest, and natural areas in the appendix on page 150. There are excellent (and free!) brochures available describing hiking and biking trails, camping, archaeology, history, and the Ice-age geology of the Heritage Corridor area. Visitors guides are also available. You can pick up some information about the I & M Canal National Heritage Corridor at the Little Red Schoolhouse Nature Center in Willow Springs. (See Section 11.) Also you can write to the Heritage Corridor Visitors Bureau, 81 N. Chicago Street, Joliet Il, or call 800-926-2262.

Canoeists will enjoy the 20-mile Chicago Portage Canoe Trail from Stony Ford in Lyons to Isle a la Cache Museum in Will County which is also part of the I & M National Heritage Corridor. Call the Forest Preserve District of Cook County at 708-366-9420 for more information and a canoe trail map.

I&M Canal Bicycle Trail

In 1848, the 96-mile I & M Canal was opened from the Chicago River near Lake Michigan to the Illinois River. This water route provided the upper Midwest with access to commerce on the East Coast and changed the course of history. Chicago, rather than St. Louis, became the transportation hub of the Midwest. Today you can hike and bike along this historic route on the Forest Preserve District's 8.9-mile I & M Canal Bicycle Trail near Willow Springs.

How to get there:

Take Route 83 or Willow Springs Road south of the Des Plaines River to Archer Avenue. Take Archer northwest of Willow Springs Road for .2 mile. Turn left at Market Street. Note the large bicycle trail welcome sign. Proceed through an industrial area for .2 mile. Cross under the Willow Springs Road bridge and over the Metra railroad tracks. Park in the first lot. The second

is for Metra commuters.

The trail runs through the parking area heading both northeast and southwest. A 2.3-mile linear central segment joins together 3.3-mile loops at both ends. Heading northeast from the parking area, the asphalt trail leads through woods that have grown since use of the canal was discontinued in 1933. The trail is shady and peaceful with little traffic sounds until you approach the I-294 underpass 1.6 miles out.

Just past the interstate, the trail turns back southwest paralleling the Sanitary and Ship Canal. This segment is 20-feet wide and is

Forest Preserve District of Cook County

I & M Canal near Willow Springs.

apparently used as a service road; although I have yet to see a vehicle on it. This northern section is a 3.3-mile loop.

Back at the trailhead, take the path to the southwest. Note how soil and vegetation have filled in the canal. Also note the remnants of an old stone bridge. Nature is slowly reclaiming man's developments. An intersection at 2.3 miles out from the trailhead is another 3.3-mile loop along the canal. Taking the path to the right you will pass two railroad crossings as well as an entrance road into a chemical company. The trail ends at the Route 83 overpass and heads back northeast to the trailhead. The two loops plus backtracking on the middle section make this an 11.2-mile round-trip.

With no street crossings except for the one entrance road, and with the flat terrain, this is a good spot for beginning bicyclists or in-line skaters. The trail is clean and well-maintained as well as being quiet and peaceful most of the way. At the trailhead, note the information display about the I & M Canal. There are no restrooms or water pumps along the trail; so come prepared.

Tinley Creek Bicycle Trail

Geologists call this area the Tinley Moraine. The last glacier 14,000 years ago deposited rocks and other debris forming a ridge. The melting glacier waters flowed east into Lake Chicago, the predecessor of Lake Michigan. Today Tinley Creek flows to the north and drains into the Calumet-Sag Channel east of Palos Heights.

Tinley Creek was originally called Bachelor's Grove Creek after those who first settled the area north of 151st Street in 1833. The land sold for $1.25 per acre which enticed several single men to purchase 5-acre segments amid the tall oak groves. Today 22 miles of bicycle trail wind through the forest preserves in two sections. Several bachelors have recently been spotted on the trails.

Northern Section

Today an 18.5-mile paved asphalt path winds north from 167st Street to 131st Street where it connects with a 2-mile Palos Heights trail leading to the Lake

Katherine Nature Preserve. The majestic oak trees, ravines, lakes, and streams as well as rolling hills with some rather steep declines and ascents make this one of my favorite Chicagoland trail systems. The pathways are well laid out and user friendly with push-to-walk buttons at most road intersections.

How to get there:

You'll find several forest preserve parking areas along the way. Here I'll describe access close to the northern and southern trailheads. To park near the southern trailhead, take 167th Street west of I-57 past Cicero Avenue to the Midlothian Reservoir Preserve entrance on the north side of 167th Street. For access to the northern trailhead, take 135th Street east of Harlem Avenue (Route 43) to the Arrowhead Lake Preserve entrance on the north side of 135th Street. The trailhead is at the far end of the parking area. The trail interconnects at 131st Street with Palos Heights' asphalt path leading 2 miles north to Lake Katherine; so you could also park at the Lake Katherine Nature Preserve. (See Section 15.) Other trail access parking areas are shown on the map.

I started my first ride at the Midlothian Reservoir Preserve on 167th Street east of Tinley Park. The path to the east overlooks the twin lakes usually populated with fishermen. This short segment (.7 mile) parallels 167th Street and then heads north along Cicero Avenue to 163rd Street. Currently there is no stoplight at this busy intersection. For a safer crossing to reach a new trail in Midlothian, cross Cicero farther south at 167th Street at the stoplight. Then head north on the sidewalk along the east side of Cicero to 159th Street. At the northeast corner of the intersection is access to a new 3-mile trail that loops through the Midlothian Meadows Preserve. Construction of this trail segment was being completed at the time of writing.

After backtracking to the parking area, head west along 167th Street to Central Avenue. Use the pedestrian walk button. A .4-mile side trail continues west along 167th. The main trail heads north along the west side of Central past Yankee Woods Preserve. Note the attractive oak grove near the shelter. Here, as on much of the Tinley Creek trail, the pathway is hilly and curvy. Take your time and enjoy what nature has to offer. North of the first preserve entrance is a trail intersection. Either

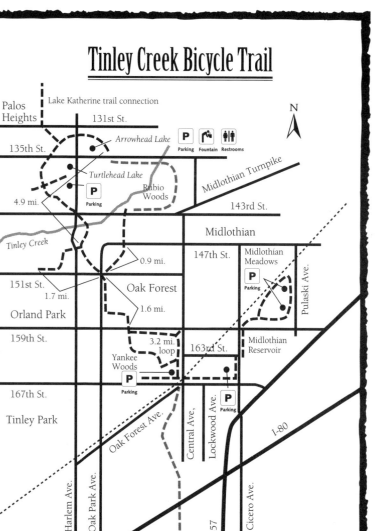

Tinley Creek Bicycle Trail

Palos Heights

Lake Katherine trail connection

131st St.

Arrowhead Lake

135th St.

P — Parking
🚶 — Fountain
🚻 — Restrooms

N

Midlothian Turnpike

Turtlehead Lake

P — Parking

Rubio Woods

4.9 mi.

143rd St.

Tinley Creek

Midlothian

147th St.

Midlothian Meadows

P — Parking

Pulaski Ave.

0.9 mi.

151st St.

1.7 mi.

Oak Forest

1.6 mi.

Orland Park

159th St.

3.2 mi. loop

163rd St.

Midlothian Reservoir

Yankee Woods

P — Parking

167th St.

Tinley Park

Oak Forest Ave.

Central Ave.

Lockwood Ave.

P — Parking

I-80

Harlem Ave.

Oak Park Ave.

I-57

Cicero Ave.

Flossmoor   Rd.

3.6 mile loop

P — Parking
▶ — Trail Access

– – – Bicycle Trail
– – – Proposed Bicycle Trail
· · · · Railroad

Vollmer Rd.

🚶 — Fountain
🚻 — Restrooms

Matteson

Yankee Woods Preserve.

direction north or west takes you on a loop around the George W. Dunne National Golf Course. (See map.) Try one route going out and the other returning. The path west is more scenic through mature woods and along the golf course. Northwest of the golf course, the main trail heads north across 159th Street. Watch for a view of the Chicago skyline 20 miles northeast as you approach Oak Park Avenue.

The next road crossing is 151st Street at the intersection with Oak Park Avenue. The path straight ahead continues northeast through mostly open field 1.7 miles to143rd Street at Ridgeland Avenue. The trail temporarily ends at the creek a short distance east of Ridgeland. Plans are to complete the loop heading northwest through the Rubio Woods Preserve to Arrowhead Lake as shown on the map. Until this portion is completed, you'll need to backtrack to 151st Street. To continue north, cross Oak Park Avenue at the stoplight. Heading northwest, you will soon come to another trail intersection. The path left (west) heads downhill through a stand of tall oaks and then proceeds through an underpass below Harlem Avenue leading into an Orland Park residential area along 151st Street. The trail ends at 82nd

Avenue next to the Silver Lake Country Club. The last .4 mile of path is actually a sidewalk along residential driveways. You may want to skip that part unless you are determined, as I was, to complete the entire trail. Probably some male idiosyncrasy!

Back at the trail intersection east of the Harlem underpass, head north (left) to continue your journey. Soon you'll pass over Tinley Creek on a huge 285-foot long bridge. The path along this beautiful area takes you past huge oaks, ravines, and gullies.

After crossing at the busy Harlem Avenue and 143rd Street intersection, the trail heads northwest. You'll soon come to a conflux of Com Ed high tension electrical lines running three different directions. Electrifying! North of the powerlines is a four-way trail intersection. The path to the right is a side trail that leads to Turtlehead Lake. The lake owes its existence to the Tri-State Tollway. Earth fill was needed to construct the highway. The pleasant side benefit was this peaceful lake. Backtrack to the trail intersection. The path straight ahead deadends in a short distance. Turn right heading north. A scenic view of Turtlehead Lake and the surrounding woodlands is to your right.

Soon you'll come to yet another trail intersection. The path to the left leads to a road crossing at 131st Street. North of 131st Street, the asphalt path leads 2 miles to Lake Katherine in Palos Heights. The path to the right (northeast) leads to Arrowhead Lake. After a crossing at Harlem Avenue, head around the lake to a picnic area which currently is the end of the trail. As mentioned above, a trail extension is planned running east through Rubio Woods Preserve which will create a loop and will eliminate the need to backtrack. Heading straight back to Midlothian Reservoir on the main trail, with no more side trails, the round-trip is approximately 39 miles including the new Midlothian Meadows trail addition.

Water pumps, picnic tables, and restrooms can be found at the Arrowhead Lake, Turtlehead Lake, Yankee Woods, Midlothian Reservoir and Midlothian Meadows Preserves.

Southern Section

West of Flossmoor is a 3.6-mile loop bicycle trail mostly through open meadow with a relatively flat terrain.

How to get there:

Take I-57 to Vollmer Road. Go east on Vollmer to the Vollmer Road Picnic Area entrance on the north side. Parking is also available on Flossmoor Road to the north.

The Forest Preserve District reforested heavily in this area in the late 1960s. The trail enters woodland areas in several spots but much of the loop is through open fields. The asphalt pathway is clean and well-maintained.

Water pumps, rustic restrooms, and picnic tables are available at the Vollmer Road parking area. There is only a water pump at the Flossmoor Road entrance.

The Forest Preserve District plans to interconnect the northern and southern sections. When complete, the Tinley Creek Bicycle Path will consist of 33 miles making it one of the premier trails in Chicagoland.

Footpaths

You'll also find footpaths intersecting with the bike path at the Vollmer Road Preserve, Midlothian Reservoir, and near Tinley Creek south of 143rd Street.

Lake Katherine Nature Preserve

The community of Palos Heights has converted an area along the Calumet-Sag Channel from a dumping ground into a 158-acre nature preserve with a large lake, prairie, wetlands, a waterfall garden, 3.3 miles of hiking trails, and an Environmental Learning Center. This work earned the preserve a 1992 National Landscaping Award presented by First Lady Barbara Bush.

How to get there:

Take Route 83 east of Route 45 or west of Harlem Avenue (Route 43) south of the Calumet-Sag Channel. The entrance is at the intersection of Route 83/College Drive and 75th Avenue/Lake Katherine Drive. On foot or bicycle, from the Tinley Creek Bicycle Trail at 131st Street, head north on the 2-mile asphalt bicycle path. (See Section 14.)

Preserve visitors will first encounter a picturesque waterfall and small rippling brook. Water from the nearby lake is pumped over to create a scenic and peaceful spot. Ducks swim in the pool at the bottom of the falls. Benches are nearby if you want to relax and enjoy. There are

Bill Banks

Waterfall at Lake Katherine.

also small conifers as well as flower and butterfly gardens nearby. Butterflies rely on specific plants to lay their eggs and feed. On a warm, windless, sunny August day, you may see hundreds of these delicate creatures sipping nectar from annual and perennial flowers planted there to attract them. A walk on the 1-mile woodchip trail around 20-acre Lake Katherine leads to an overlook of the Calumet-Sag Channel, and recent plantings of spruce, pine, and deciduous trees to reforest the area. At the western end of the lake is a short .3-mile trail through a Children's Forest. In spring 1990, children from the community and their families planted 500 trees as a major part of the reforestation effort. What a wonderful idea! Fifty years from now, those same children can bring their grandkids back to show them how they helped to restore one small piece of their natural environment.

On the east side of the lake is a nature center with displays as well as a children's theater. Educational programs are offered year-round. East of the center is the Buzz N' Bloom Prairie containing close to 100 native prairie species. A trail through the prairie leads to a foot bridge over a bubbling brook heading east to Harlem Avenue. An underpass

Lake Katherine Nature Preserve

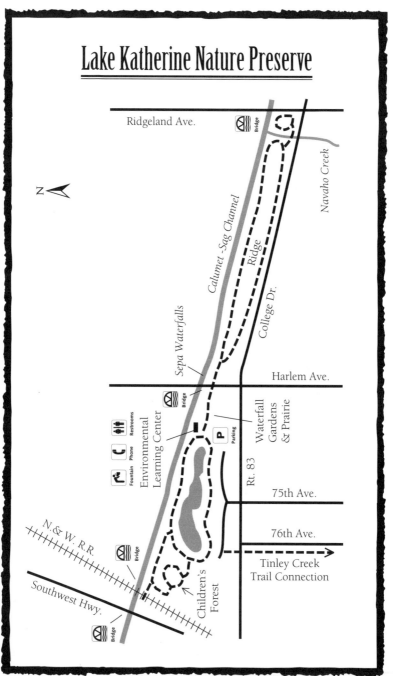

at Harlem leads to the 33-acre Eastern Preserve with 2 miles of hiking trails through woods and prairie. After crossing under Harlem, you will encounter a massive waterfall flowing into the Cal-Sag Channel. Built by the Water Reclamation District of Greater Chicago, the falls at the Worth station naturally aerate the waters of the very slow moving channel thus protecting the environment for fish and aquatic plants. One of five Sidestream Elevated Pool Aeration (SEPA) stations in the Chicago area, the Worth waterfalls really add to the enjoyment of the hike. You might also see a slow moving barge propelled eastward by a towboat heading to Calumet Harbor on Lake Michigan, the largest port on all the Great Lakes. Mississippi River barges get access to the Great Lakes and the East Coast via the Cal-Sag Channel and the Calumet River. Like its counterpart to the north, the Chicago Sanitary & Ship Canal, the Cal-Sag Channel was constructed between 1911 and 1922 to help control pollution of Chicago's drinking water by reversing the flow of the Calumet River so that it headed southwest rather than into Lake Michigan. Prior to that, a stream ran through the area. Native Americans called it the Checagou just as they did the river to the north now called the Chicago River. In fact, some south-siders dispute the conventional wisdom that Jolliet and Marquette trekked up the Des Plaines River. Rather they argue that the river that once ran where the Cal-Sag Channel now flows was more navigable and thus the preferred route by Native Americans and the true route of the early French explorers.

The 2 miles of trail in the Eastern Preserve consist of a 1-mile woodchip path paralleling the channel called the Old Canoe Path Trail. The original dredging of the channel as well as a major widening from 60 to 225 feet by the Army Corps of Engineers in 1955 left huge piles of earth and stone forming a long ridge paralleling the channel. Since then trees and plants have grown on the ridge. A 1-mile Over-look Trail serves to complete a loop back to the nature center. This trail is rugged in spots with loose stone and tree roots. Also the path-way was hard to find and follow due to overgrown vegetation. Signage is planned for 1996 and the buckthorn will be cut back to keep the trail open. I would suggest that only those with sturdy shoes and strong legs try the Overlook Trail. Beaver, coyote, and fox have been spotted as well as great-horned owl, black-crowned night heron, and many types of nesting birds. Bank swallows are being attracted to the area through the installation of clay tubes along the channel.

The trails are open for hiking only. A bike rack is available near the entrance by the community clubhouse. A drinking fountain, soft drinks, and restroom are available at the nature center. Grounds are open from dawn until 10 p.m. daily. Trails are open for cross-country skiing in winter when the snows come. Call 708-361-1873 for more information.

Thorn Creek Greenway

Thorn Creek runs through southern Cook County flowing into the Little Calumet River east of South Holland near the Sand Ridge Nature Center. Seventy-five hundred acres of Cook County Forest Preserves form a mostly continuous greenway that protects the wetlands and woodlands along the way. Two sections of the Thorn Creek Bicycle Trail meander through the forest preserves with 4.6 miles of trail west of Lansing and farther south 4.7 miles of trail east of Park Forest near the Will County border. Plans are to connect the two sections to form 17.5 miles of off-road trail.

Northern Section

The 10-foot wide paved asphalt bike path wanders through open meadows and some woodland areas. The route is mostly linear paralleling North Creek as it makes its way west to merge with Thorn Creek on the north side of Glenwood.

How to get there:

Take the Calumet Expressway to

Thorn Creek Greenway

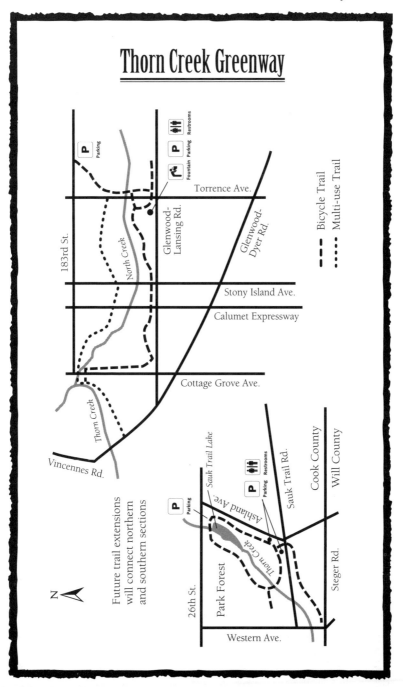

Glenwood-Dyer Road. Head east .3 mile to Stony Island Avenue. Turn left (north) on Stony Island to Glenwood-Lansing Road. Turn right (east) on Glenwood-Lansing. Turn left into the North Creek Meadow Preserve parking area. The bike path can be accessed at the far end of the parking area. The trail runs through two other nearby forest preserves with parking areas: Lansing Woods Preserve on 183rd Street east of Torrence and Sweet Woods Preserve on Cottage Grove Avenue west of the Calumet Expressway.

Heading east from the North Creek Meadow preserve parking area, there is a street crossing with a pedestrian button at Torrence Avenue. A trail intersection is east of Torrence. The northbound path to the left takes you to the Lansing Woods Preserve at 183rd Street. The eastbound path to the right ends north of Lynwood. After backtracking to the North Creek Meadow Preserve, continue west along or near Glenwood-Lansing Road. A long bridge provides a safe passage over the Calumet Expressway. As you approach Cottage Grove Avenue, the path turns north and heads to the Sweet Woods Preserve and Thorn Creek north of the community of Glenwood. Biking or hiking the entire trail is a 9.2-mile trip assuming backtracking.

Rustic restrooms, water pumps, and picnic tables can be found near the parking areas of the three preserves along the way. The trail is relatively flat with a few hills in spots. The bike path is clean and well-maintained.

Unpaved Multi-Use Trail

North of the shelter at the Sweet Woods Preserve you will find access to a 5-mile packed earth multi-use trail which runs from Vincennes Road north of Glenwood east to Torrence Avenue near Lansing. Much of the path is through woodlands often on bluffs overlooking Thorn and North Creeks. The Forest Preserve District map labels this trail "developed". That is a bit of an overstatement. The trail has mud holes, deep ruts, and tree roots. The trail is fine for hikers, mountain bikers, and equestrians but not a good choice for a road bike. You'll pass through Sweet Woods, Jurgensen Woods, and North Creek Meadow Forest Preserves along the way.

Southern Section:

Two hundred years ago, the Sauk Trail, a Native American trade route, ran from the Mississippi River to Fort Detroit on Lake St. Clair. Today the Sauk Trail Road in the southern tip of Cook County follows a part of this ancient pathway. Nearby Thorn Creek has formed Sauk Trail Lake. Here you will find a very hilly 4.7-mile asphalt bicycle path around the lake and through the woods.

How to get there:

The forest preserve trail is south of Lincoln Highway (Route 30), east of I-57 and Park Forest, and west of Dixie Highway (Route 1). Take Sauk Trail Road 1.9 miles west of Dixie Highway to Ashland Avenue. Turn right (north) and proceed .4 mile to Sauk Trail Woods Grove #6 parking area entrance on your left (west).

The beginning is characteristic of most of the trail—a lengthy climb through a mature woods with little traffic sounds. A side trail to the right leads to 26th Street. Turning west, the main path crosses over Thorn Creek before it empties into Sauk Lake. West of the lake, you'll travel through several oak groves. Another side trail to the right leads to the community of Park Forest. The main trail heads back east again crossing Thorn Creek to complete a 3.2-mile loop. Take the next path to the right to cross over Sauk Trail Road. Use the pedestrian button at the stoplight. South of Sauk Trail, the trail heads southwest to Steger Road and the Will County line. Along the trail, south of Sauk Trail Road, the home of Revolutionary War veteran John McCoy once stood. Later the site became a stop on the "Underground Railway" for former slaves. Leaving the forest preserve, the path continues a short distance along Steger Road. I found quite a bit of glass strewn on the asphalt path along Steger Road, so if you're returning to the forest preserve, you may want to avoid this part.

Inside the preserve the pathway is clean and well-maintained. Trail usage was light to moderate on my visit. There are rustic restrooms, picnic tables and a water pump at the Sauk Trail Woods Forest Preserve. The Forest Preserve District intends to connect the northern and southern sections of the Thorn Creek Bicycle Path with an 8.2-mile addition paralleling the creek through Glenwood, Flossmoor, and Chicago Heights.

Sand Ridge Nature Center

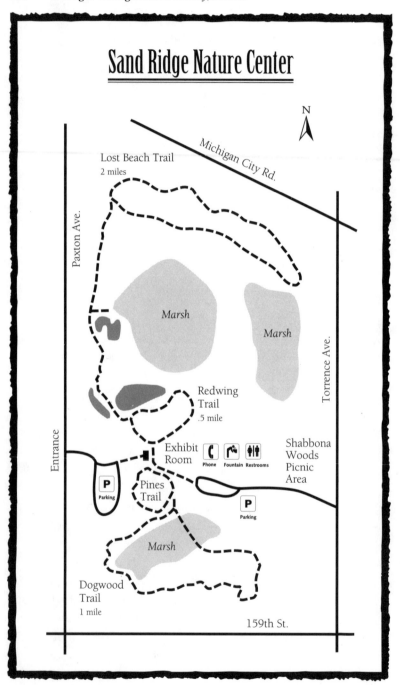

Forest Preserve District of Cook County

A family hike at Sand Ridge.

Sand Ridge Nature Center

The melting waters of the last glacier formed Lake Chicago which covered most of present day Cook County. As the waters sculpted rivers and creeks, the lake level gradually dropped forming continuously changing shorelines. Prairies and forests evolved and flourished on ridges created by the melting waters. Wetlands formed in the low areas between the ridges. The Sand Ridge Nature Center, in South Holland, is located on a ridge of what was once the shoreline of Lake Chicago, a much larger version of today's Lake Michigan.

How to get there:

Take Torrence Avenue (Route 83) to 159th Street (Route 6). Head west on 159th for .5 mile. Turn right on Paxton Avenue. Head north for .4 mile to the Nature Center entrance on the right.

Four hiking trails here offer a quiet walk through woods and marshes. The Pines Trail is a .3-mile loop starting in front of the nature center building which connects with the Dogwood Trail, a 1-mile loop trail. The trails have a mostly packed-earth surface with woodchips or mowed turf in spots. Note the tall stand of basswood trees and the "Pee Wee" prairie. The trail leads through a large marsh. In the spring, you can see trillium, wild geranium, blue phlox and other wildflowers blooming. Information signposts describe the restored prairie as well as offer facts about the white oak, Illinois' state tree, and the 20,000 species of insects that live in Cook County. Bring mosquito spray in summer.

Behind the nature center building is a small garden filled with plants that attract butterflies in the summer. Nearby is the Sandridge Settlers area. Several log cabins depict how the early settlers lived in the 1830s. Not one TV, car, or even a bicycle!

The trailhead for the Redwing and Lost Beach Trails is east of the cabins. The Redwing Trail is a .5-mile loop that passes through an oak forest near a large pond. A bull frog serenaded me on an early July hike as an American goldfinch fluttered nearby. The Lost Beach Trail is a bit more rugged than the others. A .5-mile path heads north to a 1-mile loop. A very long boardwalk runs through a marsh. The white cottonwood seed pods floating on the water mixed with the green algae and lent a "Christmasy" look to the wetlands.

After the boardwalk, the trail surface is filled with chunks of sandstone that make for rougher hiking. Also the trail becomes very narrow and overgrown in spots. On the Lost Beach Trail you will encounter a signpost that describes 8,000 year-old Toleston Beach. Here Lake Chicago waters once lapped at the sandy beach in what was then a dunesland area. Remnants of the beach are visible in the sand residue left on the trail.

You will find numerous nature displays, as well as restrooms, a drinking fountain, and a public telephone at the nature center. The Forest Preserve District offers year-round programs. Call 708-868-0606 for more information.

Chicago Park District Bikeway

If you are looking for beautiful lake vistas and great people watching, this path is the place for you. On a nice spring day, the lakefront bicycle path is a stream of humanity on the move, either on bicycles, on rollerblades, or walking or running. You'll encounter hundreds of path users over the 18.5-mile route. Solitude and serenity can be found near the path while enjoying some great panoramic views of the Chicago skyline and Lake Michigan. Along the way, there are five city parks, Burnham, Calumet, Grant, Jackson, and Lincoln as well as 31 beaches.

How to get there:

The bike path lies east of and parallels Lake Shore Drive for almost 18 miles from Bryn Mawr Avenue to 67th Street Beach on the south side of Chicago where the two part company. From 67th Street the path first heads east to South Shore Beach and then south to its southern terminus at 71st Street at the South Shore Cultural Center. The northern trailhead is at Ardmore Avenue in the Rogers Park neighborhood. As the path heads south, the best parking is east of Lake Shore Drive in the parks along Lake Michigan near the following intersecting streets: Foster, Lawrence, Montrose, Irving Park, Belmont, and Fullerton. South of the Loop and Grant Park, exit off of Lake Shore Drive at Roosevelt Road, 31st Street, 47th Street, 63rd Street, or 71st Street. Bring quarters to use the metered spaces.

There are many pedestrian tunnels and bridges under or over Lake Shore Drive along the way. Also on bicycle, the lakefront bike path can be reached from the Evanston Bikeways. From the bike path along the southern city limits of Evanston, by the Calvary Cemetery, follow the bike route signs through Rogers Park. (See Section 19.)

The entire pathway is relatively flat with small knolls at only a few spots (Lincoln Park and Montrose Harbor areas). The bike path is divided by a yellow line down the middle to segregate north and southbound traffic. White stripes on the edges provide some room for walkers and runners and define the trail. A separate crushed limestone path runs parallel to the asphalt- or concrete-surfaced bike path for part of the way. Given the many trail users, extra caution and courtesy is essential. Take your time and enjoy. Mileage markers every 1/2 mile measure your progress. You will find beaches, water fountains, concession stands (in season), picnic tables, bike racks, public telephones, and restrooms at many spots along the way. Remember the weather person's favorite phrase "cooler near the lake". In spring and fall, that usually means bring along a jacket.

Given the location, points of interest are innumerable. Just a few have been listed on the map. To whet your appetite, let's take a trip on the path starting at the northern terminus near Hollywood Beach. Heading south the path is a 12-foot wide concrete surface. Stay to the right. You'll pass Foster Avenue Beach followed by Montrose Beach and Montrose Harbor in the second mile. Waveland Golf Course is to the left south of Montrose Harbor. Nearby is the Magic Hedge, a mecca for bird watchers during spring and fall migration. Early mornings in May you'll find hoards of people with binoculars hovering around this special group of shrubs and trees. This greenery along the lakefront attracts migrating songbirds which, exhausted from their

Chicago Park District

Buckingham Fountain

night's journey, drop into the shrubs for rest and to find insects for breakfast. Note the totem pole and the Chicago Yacht Club Belmont Station to your right as you continue south.

In the summer, you can take in a play at the Theatre on the Lake east of the path at Fullerton Avenue. For an interesting detour to the west also at Fullerton, you'll find the Lincoln Park Conservatory and Lincoln Park Zoo. Admission is free! Head west on the sidewalk along Fullerton Avenue under Lake Shore Drive for .3 mile to Cannon Drive. Head south to the zoo entrance. The conservatory is west of the zoo. Across the street from the zoo is the Lincoln Park Cultural Center which offers recreational, educational and cultural programs.

Back on the lakefront pathway, you'll find some great scenic views of the downtown area, including the recently refurbished Navy Pier, starting around Fullerton Avenue. At 6.4 miles out near North Avenue Beach is a chess pavilion where you'll find players deep in concentration trying to ignore the many passersby. You'll know when you are approaching North Avenue Beach, as the path becomes increasingly congested. Be prepared to stop at any moment as rollerbladers fall,

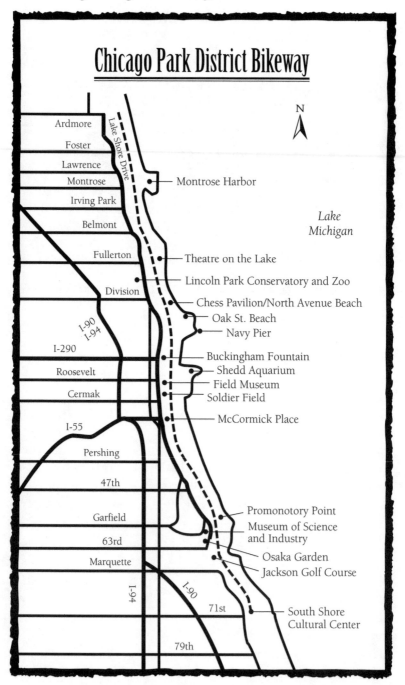

Chicago Park District Bikeway

N

Ardmore
Foster
Lawrence
Montrose
Irving Park
Belmont
Fullerton
Division

Lake Shore Drive

Montrose Harbor

Lake
Michigan

Theatre on the Lake
Lincoln Park Conservatory and Zoo
Chess Pavilion/North Avenue Beach
Oak St. Beach
Navy Pier

I-90
I-94
I-290
Roosevelt
Cermak
I-55
Pershing
47th
Garfield
63rd
Marquette

Buckingham Fountain
Shedd Aquarium
Field Museum
Soldier Field
McCormick Place

Promonotory Point
Museum of Science
and Industry
Osaka Garden
Jackson Golf Course

I-94
I-90
71st
79th

South Shore
Cultural Center

young children chase a ball, or others stop in the middle of the path for a conversation. To the south is popular Oak Street Beach. In the summer, the crowds fill the beach, the path, sidewalks, and any other available spots.

At 7.9 miles out, you'll pass Ohio Street Beach before you reach Navy Pier. Sandwiched between the beach and the pier is a nice surprise. In Olive Park, you'll find a short promenade heading east for a short distance. Two overlook areas offer great views of Lake Michigan, Ohio Street Beach, and the city behind it.

Next comes a real "happening" place to coin a phrase from my long ago youth. Navy Pier offers a beautiful fountain near the entrance, street musicians, restaurants, a carousel, tour boats, a beer garden, and many other amusements. At the trail intersection in the newly established Jane Addams Park, go left to head out to Navy Pier or right to continue south on the lakefront path. Bicyclists are allowed on the promenade in the pier area. Follow the bike route signs along Streeter Drive past Grand Avenue. I would suggest going very slowly or walking your bike with the crowd of pedestrians. It's certainly worth a stop. Bike racks are available. The farther out on the pier the less the human traffic. At the end of the pier, I enjoyed watching the sail boats float by the lighthouse.

To continue south on the lakefront path, head west to the bike route sign in front of the Lake Point Tower complex. The bike path continues south on a sidewalk next to an auto underpass at George Halas Drive. Lake Shore Drive runs on the road above you. This is a confusing congested area, so be particularly cautious. Here the path crosses over the Chicago River where it empties into Lake Michigan. A few blocks west, a short time ago in the early 19th century, Fort Dearborn stood as the only early settler-made structure within miles.

South of the river is Grant Park where you will find the Art Institute, the Adler Planetarium, Shedd Aquarium, the Field Museum of Natural History, the Petrillo Bandshell where the Grant Park Music Festival offers free outdoor concerts in the summer, and beautiful Buckingham Fountain. Pedestrian traffic is extremely heavy in this area. Use the pedestrian button to cross over Lake Shore Drive for a closer look at Buckingham Fountain. Built in 1927, and fully restored in 1995, the world's largest fountain shoots jets of water 150 feet into the sky. At night a computer controlled multi-colored light show enhances the fountain's beauty. New pavilions will offer restrooms, concessions, and other amenities. A bit farther south take another short detour out to the planetarium. Bike racks are available. Buy a hot dog from a street vendor and have lunch in the shade of the mowed grass area on the north side of the auto road. Here you'll find one of Chicago's best views, the boats floating in the harbor, Grant Park, and the bustling Loop. With all the great attractions/distractions downtown, it's hard to stay on the trail but here goes! Next you'll pass by Soldier Field, home of the Chicago Bears, Meigs Field airport, and huge McCormick Place, the world's largest exposition center.

South of McCormick Place the path is less congested. Much of the remaining distance is through grassy areas along the lake starting with Burnham Park near 47th Street. Soon you'll come to woodsy Promonotory Point designed by Daniel Burnham, primary architect of the Chicago parks. Here you'll find another great view of Lake Michigan and the city's skyline. Just south of Promontory Point is the prestigious Museum of Science and Industry, Chicago's most visited attraction. Next comes Jackson Park with a beach and 18-hole golf course. The path leaves its faithful companion, Lake Shore Drive, at 67th Street and heads east to the South Shore Beach. The pathway ends near the South Shore Cultural Center at 71st Street. The center offers theater, jazz music, a nine-hole golf course, tennis courts, and cultural programs.

The Chicago lakefront path is unlike any other in the Chicago area. While you won't find many secluded nature areas, you will find much of what makes Chicago a great place for tourists from all over the world. For a more detailed map of the path, call the Chicago Park District at 312-747-2474.

North Park Village Nature Center

A 61-acre site on Chicago's northside is being restored to its natural state by the city's Department of Environment. The only nature center in Chicago is at North Park Village. You can hike through 2.5 miles of forest, wetlands, and prairie. As you walk the trails, you might see green-backed or great blue herons, fox, and, more commonly, deer.

How to get there:

Take Peterson Avenue east of I-94 to Pulaski Road. Head south .2 miles to North Park Village. Drive past the guard station and go left at the stop sign following the road to the nature center.

Eighty-five years ago this land contained a farm and nursery. In 1911, the city built a sanitarium here for tuberculosis patients. You will find some old concrete sidewalks along the woodchip trails from those days. In 1974, the sanitarium, no longer needed, was closed. A conservation easement protected the site from further development. Today a retirement community fills a sizable part of the former sanitarium grounds. But the rest is being restored to woods, prairie, and wetland. A 10-foot wide woodchip trail loops through an

North Park Village Nature Center

oak savanna, along a pond, and on a boardwalk over a marsh area. Northwest of the marsh you'll find one of the preserve's highlights, a box elder tree, 13-foot wide, guarding the trail. Pancake-shaped mushrooms grow out of the gnarled trunk's crevices. Alas, this 80-120-year-old masterpiece of nature is nearing the end of its existence, since box elders typically don't live that long. Campfires are often held at the tree's base in the evening. What a great spot for story telling!

Farther west the trail leads to the Bluebird Prairie. Tallgrass species such as Indian grass grow to 6 feet or taller in the fall. In the spring, bluebirds have been seen here. Interpretive signs can be found to describe the natural heritage of the ecosystems present here.

Box Elder along the trail.

Inside the nature center you can meet "Shypoke" a green-backed heron who, due to an injury, could not be released back into the wild. Also you'll discover snakes, turtles, and toads. Kids love this place. As the only nature center in the city, North Park Village is a precious gem. The Department of Environment is currently investigating potential nature center sites. Hopefully this will result in the preservation of other Chicago natural areas.

Hours are 10 a.m. to 4 p.m. daily. Drinking water, restrooms, and a public telephone can be found at the nature center. A bike rack is available near the entrance. No pets please. Programs are offered year-round. Call 312-744-5472 for more information.

Evanston Bikeways

The first suburb north of Chicago is Evanston, home of Northwestern University. With a vibrant downtown area near the university, you will discover much to do and see here. Evanston is a bicycle-friendly community with tree-lined streets and several parks along Lake Michigan's shores. There are off-road pathways along the lakefront and the North Shore Channel as well as on-road bicycle routes. Bicycle racks are available throughout the downtown area.

Lake Shore Pathway

A 5-mile off-road route loops around Northwestern University and follows the Lake Michigan shore heading south to Chicago.

How to get there:

Take Church Street east through downtown Evanston to Sheridan Road near Lake Michigan. Park south of the university on the street along Sheridan. There is 3-hour free parking along Centennial Park. If you're planning a longer excursion, park farther south at Clark

Square Park at Kedzie Street and Sheridan.

North of Centennial Park, the bike path runs along Lake Michigan on the east side of the Northwestern University campus. A bridge over a lagoon leads to beautiful views of both the downtown Chicago skyline to the south as well as the Northwestern campus. The off-road path runs north to Lincoln Street. Head west to Sheridan Road. The sidewalk on the east side of Sheridan serves as the bike path north to Ridge Road and south to Centennial Park. This section can be quite congested when school is in session.

A short distance north of the university you'll come to the Grosse Point Light Station and Lighthouse Park. The lighthouse was built in 1873 to remedy the dangerous condition caused by shallow shoals and turbulent wind conditions off the point where many ships had sunk in Lake Michigan. The visitor/maritime center is open on weekends. Here you will find a dune restoration and wildflower garden. The lighthouse is open for tours on weekends. Call 847-328-6961. Next door is the Evanston Art Center which exhibits contemporary art.

Also a 2-mile on-road bike route beginning at the intersection of Sheridan Road and Lincoln Street will take you to the Green Bay Trail in Wilmette. (See Section 20.) Head west on Lincoln, north on Asbury Avenue, west on Isabella Street, north on Poplar Avenue, and west on Forest Avenue to Shorewood Park in Wilmette.

Parallel bicycle and pedestrian pathways run south along Lake Michigan for 1 mile from the Northwestern campus through Centennial Park and several others to Greenleaf Street. In warm weather, sailboats and seagulls quietly glide by. Following a couple of blocks of on-road route, the off-road pathway picks up again for a short distance to Sheridan Square. A sidewalk along the east side of Sheridan Road runs between Calvary Cemetery and Lake Michigan. Water fountains, picnic tables, and restrooms are available in Centennial Park.

Three and six-tenths miles to the south of Evanston's city limits is the northern terminus for the 18.5-mile Chicago Park District Bikeway. (See Section 17.) Follow the designated bike route signs along the way through the Rogers Park area.

Evanston Connection to Chicago Lakefront Bicycle Path

Southbound from Evanston Bikeways:

1) From the sidewalk east of Sheridan Road by Calvary Cemetery take Rogers Avenue .3 mile southwest to Ashland.
2) Take Ashland south to Pratt.
3) Head east (left) one block on Pratt to Bosworth.
4) Head south (right) on Bosworth .5 mile to Devon.
5) Head east on Devon one block to Greenview.
6) Head south (right) on Greenview to Granville.
7) Head east on Granville to Winthrop.
8) Head south (right) on Winthrop .5 mile to Ardmore.
9) Head east (left) on Ardmore to access the bike path.

Northbound from Chicago lakefront bikepath:

1) Take Ardmore west to Kenmore.
2) Take Kenmore north (right) to Granville.
3) Take Granville west (left) to Glenwood.
4) Take Glenwood north (right) to Arthur.
5) Take Arthur west (left) to Greenview.
6) Take Greenville north (right) to Pratt.
7) Briefly head east on Pratt to the continuation of Greenview heading north.
8) Take Greenview to Rogers.
9) Take Rogers east (right) to the sidewalk along Lake Michigan heading north by Calvary Cemetery.

North Shore Channel

The North Shore Channel connects to Lake Michigan at Wilmette Harbor north of Evanston. From there it runs south 7.5 miles to a merger with the North Branch of the Chicago River south of Foster Avenue in Chicago. Through the years since its construction in 1910, trees have grown tall along the banks. Today there is a 3-mile asphalt trail running east of the Channel through Evanston and Skokie.

How to get there:

Take Main Street in Skokie east of Route 41 to McCormick

Boulevard. Head north on McCormick and turn right into the Skokie North Shore Sculpture Park parking area.

A multi-use path runs along the west bank of the North Shore Channel .8 mile south to Oakton and 2 miles north to Green Bay Road. There are a series of overlapping loops of the asphalt pathway passing several contemporary sculptures along the way. Farther north, in Evanston, you'll find the Ladd Arboretum and the Ecology Center. Here the trail narrows and has a crushed-limestone surface. You'll find a friendship garden, bird sanctuary, small prairie demonstration area, and a windmill demonstrating alternative energy sources along the trail. Call 847-864-5181 for more information.

There are also approximately 2 miles of asphalt path along the east side of the North Shore Channel running through an urban residential area of Evanston which I did not visit.

Call the City of Evanston office at 847-328-2100 to receive a copy of the Evanston Bikeways brochure which contains a map showing both on-road and off-road bike routes. The Chicagoland Bicycle Federation's "Chicago Bicycling Map" described in the introduction contains a map depicting the Evanston and Chicago lakefront trail connections.

Green Bay Trail

In the early 19th century, travelers used an old Indian ridge trail to journey from Fort Dearborn in Chicago to Fort Howard in Green Bay, Wisconsin. On foot the trip took one month. The present Green Bay Trail is a lot shorter, approximately 18 miles from Shorewood Park in Wilmette to Lake Bluff in Lake County. Built on the right-of-way of the departed Chicago North Shore Milwaukee Railway, the Green Bay Trail parallels the Metra North Line (C & NW) railroad tracks as well as Green Bay and Sheridan Roads.

How to get there:

Since this is a Cook County guide, we'll first describe locations near the southern trailhead and northern county border. The southern trailhead is in Shorewood Park at Forest Avenue in downtown Wilmette, one block east of Green Bay Road. Park in the designated areas along Green Bay Road or Lake Street one block south. During weekdays, there is a two-hour parking limit. There is also restricted parking near the train station in Kenilworth (at Kenilworth Avenue) and Glencoe (north of Park Avenue). Farther north you can park in Turnbull Woods Forest Preserve just south of Lake Cook Road on Green Bay Road, although this requires riding or walking north along busy Green Bay Road for .2 mile. From Green Bay head right (east) .2 mile to the Braeside train station. If spaces are available, you can park free near the train station for two hours. For access near the north end of the Green Bay Trail in Lake County, take Route 176 east to Sheridan Road. Park in downtown Lake Bluff anywhere near the train station where the trail entrance is located.

The 6.2-mile Cook County portion of the trail heading north from Shorewood Park takes you through the picturesque North Shore communities of Wilmette, Kenilworth, Winnetka, and Glencoe. The well-maintained trail leads through or near a series of parks including Shorewood, Sheldon, and Veteran's Memorial as well as several community train stations. The surface is asphalt for the first few miles with a few street crossings. The path is mostly a dedicated off-road trail except for the interludes at each community's train station where you'll need to use the street or parking lot. The dedicated trail begins again at the far end of each train station's parking area. In Kenilworth near the train station, watch for the bike route signs. North of the train station, the trail proceeds through a park and then a few blocks on the street. The off-road path begins again at Ivy Court with a 180 degree "U" curve going up a small incline. Be careful here. Heading north you'll find a recently resurfaced 9-foot wide asphalt trail with a narrow crushed limestone surface to the right for runners or walkers. The next 3-mile stretch is free of road crossings due to a series of road bridges over both the Metra tracks and the Green Bay Trail. Just south of the Hubbard Woods train station is an unmarked underpass at Tower Road. Note the asphalt path climbing up the embankment to the right of the trail. For a brief side trip, take the path up the hill and head right to Tower Road. You'll find Winnetka's Tower Road Park .3 mile east along Lake Michigan. As well as a water fountain, bike racks are available if you want to walk down the long winding stairs to the beach.

Green Bay Trail

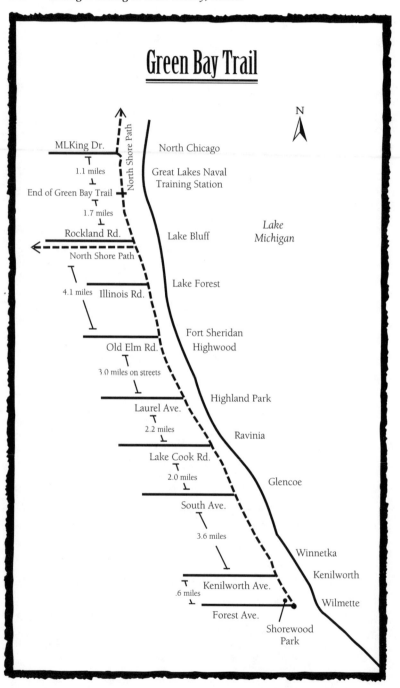

N

MLKing Dr.

1.1 miles

End of Green Bay Trail

1.7 miles

Rockland Rd.

North Shore Path

4.1 miles   Illinois Rd.

Old Elm Rd.

3.0 miles on streets

Laurel Ave.

2.2 miles

Lake Cook Rd.

2.0 miles

South Ave.

3.6 miles

Kenilworth Ave.

.6 miles

Forest Ave.

North Shore Path

North Chicago

Great Lakes Naval
Training Station

*Lake
Michigan*

Lake Bluff

Lake Forest

Fort Sheridan
Highwood

Highland Park

Ravinia

Glencoe

Winnetka

Kenilworth

Wilmette

Shorewood
Park

In Glencoe, the trail is on-road (or sidewalk if you prefer) near the train station. Here Green Bay Road is a lightly used side street through the train station parking area with Glencoe Road serving as the main auto traffic route to the west of the trail. North of downtown Glencoe, the path runs through a shady tunnel of trees with Lake Shore Country Club to the east. This is a quiet, peaceful portion of the trail with only faint road sounds. Here the surface changes to crushed limestone.

The Green Bay Trail enters Lake County in Highland Park at the Braeside train station just south of Ravinia at Lake Cook/County Line Road. (See Section 21 for a description of the connection to the Chicago Botanic Garden.) Heading north into Lake County, the surface is crushed limestone. About 1 mile north of Lake Cook, you'll come to the Ravinia train station. For a short side trip, head east on Roger Williams Avenue past Jens Jensen Park. The park is named for Jens Jensen, a renowned landscape architect who worked in Chicago and the northern suburbs to design backyard landscapes with native plants.

After .8 mile, you'll come to Rosewood Beach Park where a scenic view amid the trees on a high bluff overlooking Lake Michigan awaits you. A bike rack is available. Nearby is a stone stairway winding its way through the trees down to the beach. A very pretty spot! You'll then need to backtrack to the train station to continue north on the Green Bay Trail. The off-road trail temporarily ends at the downtown Highland Park train station at the intersection of St. John's and Laurel Avenues.

To continue take St. John's north to Central Avenue. Turn right (east) to Sheridan Road. Turn left (north) on Sheridan. Three-quarters of a mile from Central Avenue you'll pass Moraine Park. You may want to stop here for drinking water, restrooms, picnic areas, and a lovely view of Lake Michigan. Follow the signs for Sheridan Road north into Highwood by way of Edgecliff Drive, Oak Street, and Walker Avenue.

Fort Sheridan, the closed U. S. Army base is on your right. Part of this land will become a forest preserve with trails through the deep woods and along the bluffs overlooking Lake Michigan. Continue north along Sheridan Road using the sidewalk that runs in front of the former army base property. After traveling 3 miles through Highland Park and Highwood, you'll come to the Fort Sheridan train station at the intersection of Old Elm Road and Sheridan Road north of High-wood. The off-road bike trail starts up again here north of the train station parking lot. The asphalt pathway is sandwiched between the Metra train track on the left and Sheridan Road on the right. This part of the trail up to downtown Lake Forest was recently resurfaced. As you travel north into Lake Forest, you'll pass Barat College. You'll have only one street crossing between Old Elm and downtown Lake Forest. A bridge over Illinois Road leads to the train station parking lot.

At the first stop sign at Deerpath and McKinley Roads, you have three pleasant alternatives—1) Turn left across the track at the train station and explore the Market Square area. Built in 1916, Market Square was the nation's first shopping center. Architectural genius Howard Van Doren Shaw designed the square with a fountain as one of its focal points. You need to walk your bicycle in downtown Lake Forest. 2) Turn right on Deerpath Road and ride 1 mile to Forest Park to enjoy scenic bluff views of Lake Michigan. You'll find bike racks by the stairs to the beach. A long elevated boardwalk winds its way through the trees to the shoreline. You can also take a short hike on the brick walkway along the Lake Michigan beach. 3) Continue on the Green Bay Trail proceeding north through the train station parking area along McKinley. A bridge over Woodland Road from the north end of the train station parking lot leads to the off-road trail.

From downtown Lake Forest you have a 1.7-mile ride to downtown Lake Bluff. On the way you'll pass Lake Forest High School, a Georgian style building that you may remember from the movie "Ordinary People." There are two Y intersections on the trail right before you go over the bridge to the Lake Bluff train station. Either of the two paths to the left take you to a 5.5-mile bikeway paralleling Route 176 heading west. This is the west branch of the North Shore Path. Proceed straight ahead at the Lake Bluff train station to continue north on the Green Bay Trail.

There is an asphalt surface for 1.7 miles north of the train station to the city limits. The Green Bay Trail ends there and the North Shore Path starts. The surface is concrete as you enter North Chicago for 1.1 miles. To your right is the Great Lakes Naval Training Center. To continue north, turn left at Martin Luther King Drive. Proceed west two blocks to Commonwealth Avenue. Head north (right) on Commonwealth following the "Bike Path" signs. The off-road North Shore Path starts at Boak Park one block north of Broadway Avenue. There are 17 street crossings through urban areas of North Chicago and Waukegan between Broadway and Yorkhouse Roads. North of Waukegan, except for another urban section in Zion, the crushed limestone path leads through a rural, bucolic environment to 89th Street in Kenosha, Wisconsin.

The North Shore Path, from North Chicago to Kenosha is a 15.4-mile one-way trip. Add that to the 18-mile Green Bay Trail, the out-and-back from Wilmette is approximately 67 miles.

If you're hungry, there are many restaurants to sample along the way. Also you'll find water fountains, benches, and picnic tables at several of the parks. Most of the community train stations have restrooms and public telephones.

Chicago Botanic Garden

The Chicago Botanic Garden, a living museum of plants, is at Cook County's northern border. Here visitors can walk through a Japanese garden of well-manicured miniature shrubs, an English-walled garden fragrant with spring-blooming crab apple trees, a bulb garden bursting with summer lilies and autumn crocuses, and 16 other picturesque gardens along 7 miles of pathways. Due to the great diversity of plants and habitats, bird life is plentiful here especially during migration.

The 385-acre garden, owned by the Forest Preserve District of Cook County and managed by the Chicago Horticultural Society, contains 7,000 plant species including trees and shrubs.

How to get there:

The main entrance is on County Line (Lake Cook Road) .4 mile east of U.S Route 41. Parking costs $4 per vehicle. Admission is free. A good incentive to hike or bike! From the Green Bay Trail at

Chicago Botanic Garden

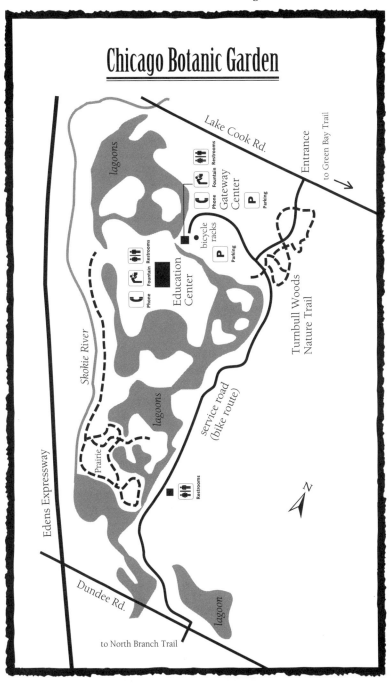

Chicago Botanic Garden

Waterfall Garden

Braeside train station (see Section 20), you can bike or walk on the sidewalk on the north side of Lake Cook Road .6 mile to the main entrance where there is a stoplight for safe crossing. The Garden can also be accessed from the south on bike or on foot through a walking-only entrance on Dundee Road just east of U.S. Route 41. This path is the North Branch Bicycle Trail. (See Section 22.) If you visit the park on your bicycle, there are racks near the entrance to the gateway center. Bikes are not allowed on the garden trails. Self-guided tour maps describing walks ranging from .3 mile to 2-miles long are available at the gateway center. In the northeastern corner of the Garden is the Turnbull Woods Nature Trail. Naturalists are restoring an oak woodlands here. The woodchip trail meanders through the woods. Secluded to the side, the nature trail is usually less crowded than the rest of the gardens. In the spring, wildflowers blanket the forest floor.

The longest walk is to the prairies in the garden's south section. Naturalists are restoring six different types of prairie communities: fen, gravel hill, mesic (tall grass), sand, savanna, and wet. Signposts explain the attributes of each prairie such as the fact that big blue stem thrives in a mesic prairie. The signposts also contain information on how Native Americans and early settlers used specific plants for medicinal purposes. Naturalists planted 50 bur oak trees in 1982 to simulate a native savanna.

The Botanic Garden serves as the trailhead for the 19-mile North Branch Bicycle Trail. One of the most scenic views in Chicagoland is on the service road that serves as a bike route through the Garden from Dundee Road to Lake Cook Road. The lagoons are visible for most of the route, but my favorite spot is overlooking the Japanese Garden and, in the background, the Waterfall Garden. Benches are nearby to sit and enjoy the view.

In the Gateway Center, an audio-visual presentation, exhibits, and wall displays provide information about the gardens. A restaurant is open for breakfast and lunch. Hours are from 8 a.m. to sunset, everyday of the year except Christmas. Many programs and activities are offered throughout the year. Call 847-835-5440 for more information.

North Branch Trails

Ten thousand years ago Lake Chicago, fed by the melting glaciers, covered what is now the North Shore. As the water level receded, a large marsh area was formed. Streams and creeks (the Skokie River, the Middle Fork, and the West Fork) flowed south through the marsh to create the North Branch of the Chicago River. The Potowatami called the marsh Chewab Skokie or "big wet prairie". Teeming with wildlife, the wetland was filled with wildflowers and tall grasses. In the 1920s, the fertile soil attracted developers who drained the marsh to use the land for growing crops. However, they did not understand the nature of the wetlands. In spring, the entire area would flood including nearby roads and residential areas. In the fall, dry peat beds would catch on fire and burn for weeks. Mosquitoes ruled.

By the 1930s, the Forest Preserve District acquired most of the land along the Skokie River. The Civilian Conservation Corps (CCC), formed during the Depression to provide work for many Americans, was charged with building a series of lagoons to stop the

Forest Preserve District of Cook County

North Branch of the Chicago River.

flooding. Two hundred men excavated four million cubic yards of dirt to create the lagoons. Dams and dikes were used to maintain the water level. The seven Skokie lagoons situated between Dundee and Willow Roads became popular recreation areas.

Over the years, however, soil erosion resulting from extensive residential and business construction filled in a significant portion of the lagoons. Beginning in the late 1980s, extensive dredging operations have restored the lagoons. Native grasses and wildflowers have been planted along the Skokie River in the Botanic Garden to help restore the wetlands.

North Branch Bicycle Trail

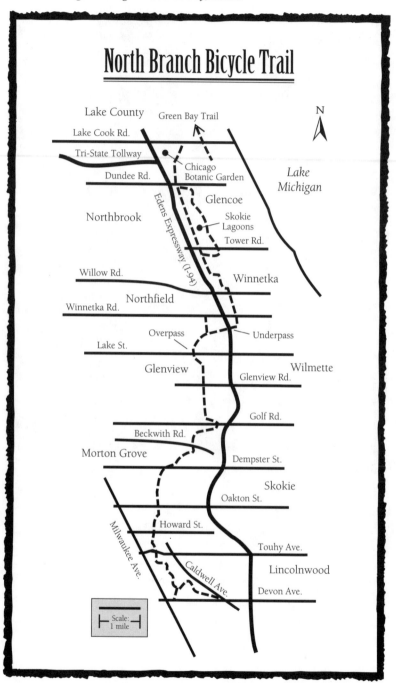

North Branch Bicycle Trail

A 19.1-mile paved asphalt bicycle trail runs along the Skokie La-goons and the North Branch of the Chicago River from the Botanic Garden at Lake Cook Road in Glencoe to Caldwell and Devon Ave-nues on the north side of Chicago.

How to get there:

To park near the southern trailhead in Chicago, take Milwaukee Avenue to Devon Avenue. Head .2 mile east to the Caldwell Woods Preserve. Take the entrance road labeled "Caldwell Woods Groves 1,2 & 3". To access the northern trailhead, take Lake Cook Road (County Line Road) to the Chicago Botanic Garden east of I-94/Route 41 and .5 mile west of Greenbay Road. See Section 21 for more information about the Botanic Garden. You can also hike or bike from the Green Bay Trail (Section 20) to the Botanic Garden. Take Lake Cook Road west for .6 mile on the sidewalk on the northside of Lake Cook Road. You'll also find many forest preserves along the way with available parking listed at the end of this section.

I will describe a trip starting at the Botanic Garden main entrance and heading south to Chicago. You cannot bike on the pathways and trails at the Botanic Garden. There is a very large bike rack area near the Gateway Center south of parking area #1. To access the bike path, follow the auto road west past the parking areas to a service road heading south. You will immediately come to one of the most gor-geous views in Chicagoland. To your right across the lake is the Water-fall and Japanese Gardens. There are benches nearby if you want to soak in the beautiful scenery.

The 1.2-mile service road leads to a crossing at Dundee Road where the bike path exits the Botanic Garden. Along the way you will pass by several gardens. There is a pedestrian button at the Dundee Road crossing.

South of Dundee a trail intersection offers paths heading both east and west of the Skokie Lagoons. The path to the right leads south along I-94 with heavy traffic sounds but also more woodland. Try one going south, the other on your return if you're doing a round-trip. The asphalt trail is clean and well-maintained with a gently rolling terrain. The next street crossing is at Tower Road 3.1 miles out (assuming you took the shorter western route along I-94). Here the two pathways merge into a single trail heading south.

Along the way, you'll pass by a boat launch area. The Skokie Lagoons area is increasingly becoming a popular waterway for canoeists. You will also notice a split rail fence separating the asphalt bike path from a paralleling gravel trail. This is a multi-use trail used by equestrians, hikers, and occasionally, mountain bikers. See description below.

The next road crossing is Willow Road at Lagoon Drive (4.7 miles out). Here the lagoons end and flow back into the Skokie River as it heads south. The bike trail separates from the river running farther west. After a crossing at Winnetka Road and a safe underpass of busy I-94, you'll come to another trail intersection. Stay to the left to keep on the main trail. You'll find a map on a signpost at the intersection. The .4-mile side trail leads back up to Winnetka Road. Nearby the Skokie River and the Middle Fork merge into the North Branch of the Chicago River. Following an overpass of Lake Street (7.1 miles out), the terrain becomes hilly and curvy. South of Lake Street, you'll pass a series of forest preserve picnic areas. Here you'll find both rustic and more modern restrooms, water pumps, picnic tables, and shelters. The trail parallels Harms Road for some distance. After road crossings at Glenview and Golf Roads (9.2 miles out), you'll pass the Northwestern Equestrian Center just south of Golf Road. Some distance west of the trail in Morton Grove the West Fork joins up to complete the North Branch of the Chicago River.

Following crossings at Beckwith Road and Dempster Street (11.2 miles out), you'll travel through the Miami Woods Prairie restoration site. South of here the trail runs through woods on a small bluff overlooking the river to the east. Following another overpass at Oakton Street, the terrain becomes even more hilly and large oak trees line the trail. There are road crossings at Howard Street and Touhy Avenue (13.8 miles out). At Touhy take the sidewalk east to the light and use the push-to-walk button. After the last crossing at Harts Road, you'll come first to the Bunker Hill and then to the Caldwell Woods Preserve picnic areas. The path right leads over a creek to the toboggan slide and on to Devon Avenue (15.2 miles out). The trail to the left runs another 1.2 miles east to the southern trailhead at Devon and Caldwell Avenue.

One-quarter million trail users bicycle, hike, run, and rollerblade on the North Branch Trail each year, so you may find a bit of a crowd in nice weather. Go slowly if you're on your bike and enjoy the scenery.

Unpaved Multi-Use Trail

An 8-mile multi-use trail runs along the river from Tower Road in Winnetka to Dempster Street/Route 14 in Morton Grove. Open to hikers, equestrians, and bicyclists, the trail is a combination of packed-earth, cinders, and crushed-limestone surface. The multi-use trail parallels the bike path for much of the route. There are a lot of roots and washouts on the trail near the river. A mountain or hybrid bike is much preferred. Also it's easy to get lost. I did at least twice! Bring a compass.

If you'd like to try a wetter route, contact the Friends of the Chicago River, a non-profit organization dedicated to preservation and restoration of the Chicago rivers. The group sponsors canoe trips during spring, summer, and fall. Call 312-939-0490 for more information.

Parking areas along the way

As well as the northern and southern trail heads mentioned above, you can also park at the following forest preserve locations:

1) Tower Road east of I-94.
2) Willow Road east of I-94.
3) Lake Avenue west of I-94.
4) Harms Road, south of Glenview Road.
5) Oakton Street west of I-94.
6) Caldwell Avenue north of Oakton Street.
7) Harts Road east of Milwaukee Avenue.
8) Caldwell Avenue south of Touhy Avenue.

Greenway Interconnecting Trails

For those of you who have read our Lake and DuPage County guidebooks, you may note that some of the following is repetitive, but keep reading to learn about exciting plans for new trails in Cook County and beyond.

For the beginner hiker or biker, 1, 2, or 5-mile trails are sufficient for getting exercise while enjoying nature. But over time many of us want to push on to adventures of longer distances over different paths and trails.

In Cook County, the rest of Chicagoland, and nationwide, significant progress is being made to interconnect existing park, forest preserve, and other trails. The term greenway is being used to identify a corridor of open land such as an old railroad or utility right-of-way or a waterway that can provide transportation for people and/or wildlife while restoring or preserving the natural environment. Often the greenway contains a trail or pathway. The Chicago River and its tributaries, Thorn, Tinley, and Salt Creeks, the lakefront, and rails-to-trails conversions, such as the Green Bay Trail and the Illinois Prairie Path, are all examples of greenways that offer trails through natural corridors. Greenways preserve and protect water and air quality and animal life as well as provide recreational opportunities and self-propelled commuting. The Chicagoland greenway system is viewed by many to be the most extensive of any metropolitan area in the country. Other greenway initiatives in Boston, New York, Seattle, and other metropolitan areas have also been successful in linking together existing parks, forests, and trails. Given the high cost of land acquisition and the scarcity of available public funds, greenways are also proving to be the most cost-effective way to provide access to open space. Old railroad right-of-ways, river flood plains, utility right-of-ways, and community developments provide opportunities for the creation of new greenways. Often the trail is surrounded by residential neighborhoods, farms, or other development. You may be able to use a greenway trail to visit a park or forest preserve on your bike rather than in your car. These linear park trails are typically much safer than the highways since contending with horses or bicycles is less risky than dealing with cars, buses, and trucks. The purpose of this section is to describe some of the activities underway to provide significantly more trails in the near future within Cook County and to interconnect with trails originating in the surrounding counties and beyond.

The Northeastern Illinois Planning Commission (NIPC) is partnering with the Chicago-based Openlands Project to coordinate the planning for an interconnected set of trails that will someday cover 1,000 miles over the six-county Chicago area. Already 450 miles of such greenways exist. With the next update to the plan, it is expected that the number of miles of greenway trails will be increased substantially. Linking these trail systems together provides an increasing interconnected and integrated trail system similar to our highway, railroad, and telephone systems.

The Northeastern Illinois Regional Greenways Plan was released in May 1993 with this purpose: " The Greenways Plan creates a vision of an interconnected regionwide network of linear open spaces that will provide benefits to northeastern Illinois — environmental, recreational, economic, aesthetic, and even transportation via trails or waterways." The plan encompasses Cook, DuPage, Kane, Lake, McHenry, and Will Counties. Greenway opportunities and priorities for development are laid out. The existing greenway network provides an excellent starting point including the major waterways (Chicago, Des Plaines, DuPage, and Fox Rivers), the Lake Michigan shoreline, old railroad routes (the Illinois Prairie Path, the Great Western Trail in DeKalb, Kane and DuPage Counties, the North Shore Path in Lake County, and the Virgil Gilman Trail in Kane County), and even old canals such as the Illinois & Michigan Canal National Heritage Corridor.

The Northeastern Illinois Greenways Plan identified the following top priorities in Cook County: Chicago Boulevard System, Chicago River (North Branch, Skokie River, West Fork), North Shore Channel, Des Plaines River, Illinois & Michigan Canal National Heritage Corridor, Lake Michigan shoreline, Green Bay Trail, Salt Creek, connections between several forest preserves and other trail systems, Centennial Trail, Illinois Prairie Path, Old Plank Road Trail, and Thorn Creek. A good example is the 20-mile Old Plank Road Trail currently under development. The first section of this rails-to-trails conversion to be completed soon will extend 12 miles from Park Forest in Cook County west to Hickory Creek Forest Preserve in Will County. Eventually Old Plank Road trail will be extended west to Joliet and also connect with the Thorn Creek Bicycle Trail.

Recently another major greenways-related initiative, CitySpace—An Open Space Plan for Chicago, has been announced.

CitySpace

In October 1995, an extensive draft CitySpace Plan was released for public review and comment. "A collaborative effort of the City of Chicago, the Chicago Park District, and the Forest Preserve District to develop a comprehensive open space plan for Chicago", the plan recognizes people's need for substantially more greenways for hiking and biking trails in the city. Creation of greenways along the Chicago River, the North Shore Channel, the Sanitary and Ship Canal, and Lake Calumet are proposed. Also new bike paths and nature trails along old railroad right-of-ways are recommended. Restoration of wetlands and natural areas, replacing the concrete and asphalt around schools with grass and trees, renovation and expansion of neighborhood parks are all part of the CitySpace plan.

While the CitySpace goals and recommendations will take many years to be completed, the plan has been well received in recognition that Chicago lags behind most major cities in the availability of parks, natural areas and off-road trails.

Greenways Involvement

Many other Cook County agencies are planning and implementing greenways. These include the Forest Preserve District of Cook County, the Cook County Division of Transportation, Chicago Park District, Illinois Department of Natural Resources and the following communities:

Alsip	Arlington Heights	Barrington	Bartlett
Buffalo Grove	Country Club Hills	Des Plaines	Elk Grove Village
Evanston	Flossmoor	Glenview	Hanover Park
Hoffman Estates	Homewood	Lemont	Matteson
Mount Prospect	Northbrook	Oak Forest	Oak Lawn
Olympia Field	Orland Hills	Orland Park	Palatine
Park Forest	Prospect Heights	Richton Park	Rolling Meadows
Roselle	Schaumburg	Skokie	Streamwood
Tinley Park			

The Regional Greenways and CitySpace plans provide an excellent vision and framework but community and county governments, regional agencies and organizations, federal and state governments, and private sector corporations, land-owners, and interested individuals must play a role in making the plan work. Voice your areas of interest if you'd like to be involved in making the Chicagoland greenways network happen. For more information call NIPC at 312-454-0400 and/or Openlands Project at 312-427-4256. Call 312-744-5822 for more information about CitySpace.

Interconnecting Trails in Nearby Counties

Greenway trails in nearby counties offer opportunities for extended bike rides and hikes. The Illinois Prairie Path (DuPage and Kane Counties) the Green Bay Trail, and the North Shore Path (Lake

County) are described in this guidebook. Interconnections with the following major trail systems in the western suburbs already exist or soon will via the Illinois Prairie Path:

• **Fox River Trail**—This 35-mile asphalt surfaced pathway runs along the picturesque Fox River from Aurora to Algonquin and the McHenry County border. There are four connections with the Illinois Prairie Path as described in Section 8. You will find many communities, forest preserves, museums, and other interesting points along the way. This well-maintained trail system is one of Chicago's most popular. Call the Kane County Forest Preserve at 708*-232-5980 for more information.

• **Prairie Trail**—Built on an old railroad right-of-way, 4.7 miles of asphalt surfaced pathway run through prairies and wetlands in southeastern McHenry County. The trail can be reached from the IPP via the Fox River Trail. This southern section of the Prairie Trail will be connected with an already existing northern portion to offer a 24-mile trail system extending the length of McHenry County to the Wisconsin border. Call the McHenry County Conservation District at 815-678-4431 for more information.

• **Great Western Trail**—A 17-mile crushed limestone trail runs from the west side of St. Charles in Kane County to Sycamore in DeKalb County. This rails-to-trails conversion crosses streams and wetlands. A 3.5-mile addition is planned to extend the Great Western Trail east to connect with the Fox River Trail. Call the Kane County Forest Preserve District at 708*-232-1242 for more information.

• **Virgil Gilman Trail**—An 11-mile nature trail extends from Kane County's southern border at Route 30 through Aurora and west to the Bliss Woods Forest Preserve. Along the way, the trail crosses the Fox River and Waubansee Creek. An addition will extend the path-way to the Waubansee Community College campus. Also a pathway along the river connecting the Fox River Trail with the Virgil Gilman Trail has been funded and will be constructed in the near future.

Call the Fox Valley Park District at 708*-897-0516 or the Kane County Forest Preserve District at 708*-232-5980 for more information.

*Note DuPage County and the southern half of Kane County's area code changes to 630 in August 1996.

Beyond Chicagoland

In the introduction to his book, Greenways for America, Charles E. Little describes the greenway initiatives as a "remarkable citizen-led movement to get us out of our cars and into the landscape—on paths and trails through corridors of green that can link city to country and people to nature from one end of America to the other." Little traces the origins of greenways back to architects such as Fredrich Law Olmsted, creator of Central Park in New York City. He describes examples both new and old from the Big Sur in California to the Illinois & Michigan Canal National Heritage Corridor to the Hudson River Valley Greenway in New York. The book is an excellent primer for those interested in furthering the development and interconnection of greenways.

The National Park Service, the American Hiking Society, and a coalition of individuals and many trail support organizations are partnering in an effort called "Trails for All Americans—The National Trails Agenda Project." This effort began in 1988 when the President's Commission on American Outdoors recommended the development of a nationwide network of hiking and jogging trails, bikeways, and bridle paths similar to the U.S. Interstate Highway System. Planners envision major backbone interstate trails interconnecting with state, county, and local community pathways. The hope is that most Americans would live within 15 minutes of a path that could access this national network.

Eight National Scenic and nine Historic Trails provide the major backbone network. Two examples are described below:

• **The Appalachian National Scenic Trail**—a completed 2,144-mile trail through the Appalachian Mountains from Katahdin, Maine to Springer Mountain, Georgia.

• **The Trail of Tears National Historic Trail**—follows the two routes used to move 16,000 Cherokee Indians from Tennessee to Oklahoma, in 1838 and 1839. The water route covers 1,226 miles on the Tennessee, Ohio, Mississippi, and Arkansas Rivers. The 826-mile land route starts in Tennessee, crosses through Kentucky, the southern tip of Illinois, and then Missouri before the sad saga reaches its end in Oklahoma. Development of the entire trail plan has not yet been completed.

While no National Scenic or Historic Trail runs through Cook County, a statewide effort is underway to construct a Grand Illinois Trail which will run through Chicagoland then head west to the Mississippi River and back.

The Grand Illinois Trail

So you say you want to take a really long hike or bike ride? The Illinois Department of Natural Resources (DNR) is partnering with many other agencies and organizations to develop one nearby. The Grand Illinois Trail will be more than a 475-mile loop trail system through 17 counties from the western suburbs of Chicago to the Mississippi River and back. Starting at the Chicago Portage in Lyons, the trail will use existing trail systems where available as it traverses the state to the Mississippi. Running north along the river, the Grand Illinois will follow the Great River Trail from Rock Island to Savanna. The trail will then utilize a series of lightly traveled local roads accentuating the vistas of northwestern Illinois north from Savanna through Galena to Freeport. Extensions in Lake and Cook Counties will connect to the Chicago Park District (lakefront) Bikeway and the Des Plaines River Trail in Lake County. Camping and lodging will be available along the way. Hikers and bicyclists will see parts of the state they probably have never visited before. Cross-country skiers and equestrians will also share the pathways. Trail enthusiasts will in time be able to enjoy nearby adventure vacations taking on the entire trail in a single effort or (more likely) completing one segment at a time.

Nearby existing trails such as the Illinois Prairie Path, the Illinois and Michigan Canal State Trail, the Fox River Trail, and the McHenry

The Grand Illinois Trail

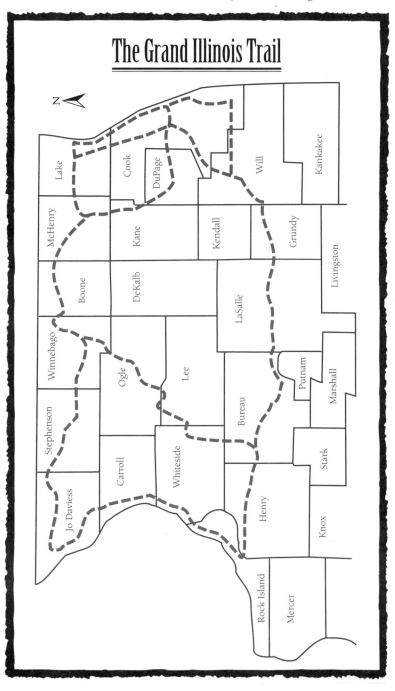

County Prairie Trail will be part of the Grand Illinois Trail. In fact, 137.5 miles of off-road trails are already in place. Projects totaling 92 miles are funded and programmed for construction, 121.5 miles of the trail route will use lightly traveled local roads and streets, and 127 miles are proposed for development. In Cook County, the Illinois Prairie Path, the Des Plaines River Trail, the Centennial Trail, the Old Plank Road Trail, the Chicago Boulevard system, the Chicago Park District Bikeway, and other proposed trails will be part of the Grand Illinois Trail. While it will take time and a major effort by the involved agencies and partnerships to construct, the Grand Illinois Trail will be an outstanding asset to trail users as well as the communities along the way.

The "Illinois State Trails Plan" published by DNR describes plans for the Grand Illinois as well as many other trails. If you are interested in finding out more, call the Illinois DNR, Division of Planning at 217-782-3715.

The Grand Illinois will connect with a new national path system, also under development, the American Discovery Trail.

American Discovery Trail

The American Hiking Society and many other agencies and organizations are partnering in the development of a 6,300-mile American Discovery Trail (ADT). Three thousand miles of trail consisting of both on and off-road routes are already marked.

From the trailhead near the Atlantic Ocean at the Cape Henlopen State Park in Delaware to the Pacific Ocean at the Point Reyes National Seashore in California, the ADT will run through urban and remote areas in 15 states and Washington D. C. Through the midwestern states including Illinois, there will be both a northern and a southern route forming a gigantic loop from Cincinnati to Denver. Open to hikers, bicyclists, and equestrians, the ADT will connect to six national scenic trails and 10 national historic trails as well as many regional and local trail systems such as ours here in Chicagoland. In northern Illinois, the ADT includes the I & M Canal State Trail, the Hennepin Canal State Trail and the Old Plank Road Trail which is currently under development. From the seashores to the deserts, to the mountains to the prairies, to the rivers and streams to the towns and cities along the way, trail users will truly be able to sample the diversity of America. Contact the American Hiking Society at 800-851-3442 for more information.

Trail User Support

Unfortunately, recent federal budget cutting initiatives in Washington have negatively impacted the progress of trails development. Some of the planned trail systems mentioned above will be delayed or perhaps never built. If you are interested in seeing the expansion of trails and off-road hiking and bicycling paths, voice your opinions to local, state, and federal government representatives particularly your U. S. House of Representatives legislators.

Appendices

Nearby Attractions

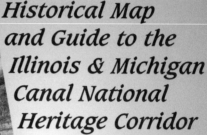

ORDER YOUR OWN...

Historical Map and Guide to the Illinois & Michigan Canal National Heritage Corridor

This full color auto driving guide is filled with maps, color photographs, and points of interest along the Illinois & Michigan Canal. It is available for purchase from the Heritage Corridor Visitors Bureau for $6.95, plus 75¢ shipping and handling.

If you would like to purchase a copy, phone 1-800-926-2262 or send a check or money order with your name and address to: Heritage Corridor Visitors Bureau, 81 North Chicago Street, Joliet, Illinois 60432.

VISA   MasterCard

Illinois & Michigan Canal National Heritage Corridor attractions are listed on pages 151 to 153.

Heritage Corridor Attractions

Historic Places

Aux Sable Aqueduct
Dellos Road at Cemetery Road
Channahon
(815) 942-0796

Chicago Portage National Historic Site
4800 S. Harlem
Lyons
(708) 366-9420

Father Marquette Memorial
St. Mary's Church
Johnson Street
Utica
(815) 667-4677

Fitzpatrick House
15701 S. Independence Blvd. (Route 53)
Lockport
(815) 740-2047

Fox River Aqueduct
I&M Canal at the Fox River
Ottawa
(815) 942-0796

Gladys Fox Museum
Ninth and Washington Streets
Lockport

Grundy County Courthouse
111 East Washington Street
Morris
(815) 942-9024

Heritage Park
Entrance at Columbia and Scott Streets
Joliet
(815) 727-8700

Illinois Appellate Court Building
1004 Columbus
Ottawa
(815) 434-5050

I&M Canal Museum and Will County Historical Society/Pioneer Settlement
803 S. State Street
Lockport
(815) 838-5080

I&M Canal Visitor Center
Gaylord Building
200 W. 8th Street
Lockport
(815) 838-4830

Jacob Henry Mansion
20 S. Eastern Avenue
Joliet
(815) 722-1420

Joliet Area Historical Society
17 E. Van Buren Street
Joliet
(815) 722-7003

LaSalle County Historical Society Museum
Route 178 and Canal Street
LaSalle
(815) 667-4861

Lemont Area Historical Society
306 Lemont Street
Lemont
(708) 257-2972
(630) 257-2972 Aug. 1996

Little Vermillion Aqueduct
I&M Canal at the Vermillion River
LaSalle
(815) 942-0796

Lock #1
I&M Canal at Division Street
Lockport
(815) 838-1183

Locks #6 & #7
At Channahon Access
Channahon
(815) 467-4271

Lock #14
Canal Street by Route 351
LaSalle
(815) 942-0796

Reddick Mansion
100 W. Lafayette Street
Ottawa
(815) 433-0084

**St. James of the Sag Church
and Cemetery**
Route 171 north of Route 83
Lemont
(708) 257-7000
(630) 257-7000 Aug. 1996

Seneca Grain Elevator
At William Street & the I&M Canal
Seneca
(815) 942-0796

Washington Park
100 LaFayette Street
Ottawa
(815) 433-0084

Points of Interest

Argonne National Laboratory
9700 S. Cass Avenue
Argonne
(708) 252-5562
(630) 252-5562 Aug. 1996

Brandon Lock & Dam
Route 6
Joliet
(815) 744-1714

Childrens' Farm at the Center
12700 Southwest Highway
Palos Park
(708) 361-3650

Dresden Island Lock and Dam
Lorenzo Road
Morris

General Fry's Landing
Stephen and River Streets
Lemont
(708) 257-1550
(630) 257-1550 Aug. 1996

Illinois State Museum Lockport Gallery
Gaylord Building
200 W. 8th Street
Lockport
(815) 838-7400

Isle a la Cache Museum
501 E. Romeo Road
Romeoville
(815) 886-1467

Joliet Park District Airport
W. Jefferson Street at I-55
Joliet
(815) 741-7267

Little Red Schoolhouse Nature Center
104th Avenue between 95th & 107th
Willow Springs
(708) 839-6897

**Metropolitan Water Reclamation
District's Deep Tunnel Pumping Station**
6001 River Road
Hodgkins
(312) 751-6633

Pilcher Park Nature Center
Gougar Road, north of Route 30
Joliet
(815) 741-7277

**Round Barn Farm Museum &
Recreation Area**
Route 52, south of I-80
Manhattan
(815) 478-3215

Slovenian Women's Union of America
431 N. Chicago Street
Joliet
(815) 727-1926

**Starved Rock Lock and Dam/Illinois
Waterway**
Dee Bennett Road
Ottawa
(815) 667-4054

**W.D. Boyce Memorial/
Ottawa Avenue Cemetery**
Ottawa Avenue & Boyce Memorial Drive
Ottawa

Will-Joliet Bicentennial Park
201 W. Jefferson Street
Joliet
(815) 740-2216

For information on these and additional attractions, call 1-800-926-2262.

Natural Areas

Buffalo Rock State Park
Dee Bennet Road
Ottawa
(815) 433-2224

Channahon State Park
Story St. or Jessup St., off Canal St.
Channahon
(815) 467-4271

Dellwood Park
State Street
Lockport, IL
(815) 838-1183

DesPlaines Valley Conservation Area
I-55 & Lorenzo Road
Wilmington
(815) 423-5326

Gaylord Donnelley Canal Trail
Between 2nd Street and Dellwood Park
Lockport
(815) 838-3313

Gebhard Woods State Park
Ottawa Street, 1 mile west of Route 47
Morris
(815) 942-0796

Goose Lake Prairie State Natural Area
N. Jugtown Road
Morris
(815) 942-2289

Hammel Woods
Black Road
Shorewood
(815) 727-8700

Heidecke State Fish & Wildlife Area
N. Jugtown Road
Morris
(815) 942-6352

I&M Canal State Trail
61 mile trail
Channahon to LaSalle/Peru
(815) 942-0796

Illini State Park
South side of Illinois River
Marseilles
(815) 795-2448

Keepataw Preserve
Bluff Road east of Joliet Road
Lemont
(815) 727-8700

Lake Katherine Nature Preserve
7607 W. College Drive
Palos Heights
(708) 361-1873

LaSalle Lake State Fish & Wildlife Area
Route 170
Marseilles
(815) 357-1608

Lockport Prairie Nature Preserve
Division St., east of Route 53
Lockport
(815) 727-8700

McKinley Woods
McKinley Road, south of Route 6
Channahon
(815) 727-8700

Matthiessen State Park
4 miles south of Utica on Route 178
Utica
(815) 667-4868

O'Hara Woods
900 W. Romeo Road
Romeoville
(815) 886-6222

Pilcher Park
Gougar Road, North of Route 30
Joliet
(815) 741-7277

Starved Rock State Park
Routes 71 & 178
Utica
(815) 667-4906

Waterfall Glen Forest Preserve
Entrances on Bluff Road and
Northgate Road
Lemont
(708) 790-4900
(630) 790-4900 Aug. 1996

W.G. Stratton State Park
Route 47, left on Illinois Avenue
Morris
(815) 942-0796

Cook County Bike Shops

You will find bike shops conveniently located near many of the trails and bike paths described in this guidebook.

Alsip
Alsip Bicycles
11600 South Pulaski Avenue
708-371-8070

Arlington Heights
ABC Cyclery, Inc.
45 South Dunton
847-253-7700

Amling's Cycle & Fitness
200 West Campbell
847-253-0349

Bikes Plus Ltd.
1313 North Rand Road
847-398-1650

Barrington
Bikes Plus
203 W. Northwest Hwy.
847-382-9200

Berwyn
Arts Cycling & Fitness
6212 West Cermak Road
708-788-0943

Dan's Bike Shop
6715 Roosevelt
708-484-5000

Brookfield
Morello's Bike Village
8827 West Ogden Avenue
708-485-6569

Buffalo Grove
Buffalo Grove Cycling & Fitness
960 South Buffalo Grove Road
847-541-4661

C. C. Cycle
307 West Dundee Road
847-541-3133

Calumet City
Calumet City Schwinn
754 Burnham Avenue
708-891-2600

Chicago
Art's Cycle
1636 East 55th Street
312-363-7524

Bike Stop
1034 West Belmont
312-868-6800

Carmen's Bike Shop
6519 West Archer Street
312-586-3247

Chicago Bicycle Company
363 West Erie Street
2nd Fl.
312-654-1796

Chicagoland Bicycle & Fitness
10126 S. Western Avenue
312-445-0811

Cycle Smithy
2468 1/2 North Clark
312-281-0444

Ed's Sports Rack
2257 East 71st Street
312-643-0505

Erehwon Mountain Outfitter
1800 North Clybourn
312-337-6400

Grand Cycle Inc.
7160 W. Grand Avenue
312-637-0944

Irv's Bike Shop
1725 South Racine
312-226-6330

Kozy's Cyclery
1610 West 35th Street
312-523-8562

Kozy's Cyclery
3712 North Halsted
312-281-2442

Kozy's Cyclery
601 South LaSalle
312-360-0020

Kozy's Cyclery
1451 West Webster
312-528-2700

On The Route Bicycle
3167 North Lincoln Avenue
312-477-5066

Oscar Wastyn Cycles
2634 West Fullerton Avenue
312-384-8999

Out Spoke'n Inc.
1400 West Belmont
312-404-2919

Performance Bicycle Shop
2720 North Halsted
312-248-0107

Quick Release Bike Shop
1623 North Halsted
312-871-3110

Rapid Transit
1900 W. North Avenue
312-227-2288

Information provided by the Chicago Area Bicycle Dealers Association

Recycle
1234 South Wabash
312-987-1080

Richard's Cycle Shop Inc.
10355 South Kedzie Avenue
312-445-3738

Rudy's Cycle & Fitness
Center
5711 West Irving Park Road
312-736-4395

Shifting Gears
4365 West Irving Park Road
312-202-8527

Sportif Importer, Ltd.
5225 West Lawrence
Avenue
312-685-0240

Turin Bicycle
435 East Illinois
312-923-0100

21st Century Cycle Ltd.
8251 West Irving Park Road
312-625-8810

Urban Bikes
1026 West Leland
312-728-5212

Village Cycle Center
1337 North Wells
312-751-2488

Wheels & Things
5210 South Harper Avenue
312-493-4326

Countryside
Terry's Byke Haus
9828 West 55th Street
708-352-4537

Dolton
Compleat Cyclist
703 Sibley Boulevard
708-841-2688

Elk Grove Village
Village CycleSport
63 Park & Shop
847-439-3340

Evanston
The Pony Shop
743 Chicago Avenue
847-864-5775

RRB Bicycles
614 Davis Street
847-733-0203

Turin Bicycle
1027 Davis Street
847-864-7660

Glenview
Glenview Schwinn
910 Waukegan Road
847-724-5790

Glenwood
Byron's Schwinn Cycling &
Fitness
315 Glenwood-Lansing
Road
708-758-4500

Hanover Park
Two Seasons Cycle & Ski
1818 West Irving Park
Road
708-213-2133

Hillside
A & J's Hillside Cyclery
4049 Washington Blvd.
708-544-7200

Hinsdale
Hartley's Cycle Shoppe Ltd.
24 West Hinsdale Avenue
708-323-7156

Homewood
Byron's Schwinn Cycling &
Fitness
18440 Governors Hwy.
708-957-9888

Kenilworth
RRB Bicycles
562 Green Bay Road
847-251-7878

LaGrange
The Wheel Thing
15 South LaGrange Road
708-352-3822

Mt. Prospect
Prospect Bike Shop
506 E. Northwest Hwy.
847-259-4569

Niles
Amlings Cycle & Fitness
8140 North Milwaukee
Avenue
847-692-4240

Village Bike Shoppe
8744 Shermer Road
847-965-7376

Northbrook
George Garner Cyclery, Inc.
1111 Waukegan Road
847-272-2100

Wheels of Northbrook
1348 Shermer Road
847-564-3700

Oak Forest
Precision Cyclery Inc.
5525 West 159th Street
708-535-0125

Oak Lawn
Otto's Cyclery
8835 South Ridgeland
708-599-7515

Oak Park
Barnard's Schwinn
6109 W. North Avenue
708-524-2660

Oak Park Cyclery
1113 Chicago Avenue
708-524-2453

Lickton's Cycle City
310 Lake Street
708-383-2130

Orland Hills
Bike Line of Orland Hills
9255 West 159th Street
708-460-4846

Orland Park
Orland Park Schwinn
Cyclery
14445 S. John Humphrey
Drive
708-460-2999

Palatine
Mike's Bike Shop
155 N. Northwest Hwy.
847-358-0948

Palos Hills
Palos Hickory Bicycle
7926 West 103rd Street
708-598-9090

Park Ridge
Bob's Bicycle Shop of Park
Ridge
141 South Vine Street
847-825-4438

Marty's
623 Devon Avenue
847-823-9307

Performance Bicycle Shop
658 N. Northwest Hwy.
847-823-5116

Prospect Heights
Power Motions
3 East Camp McDonald
847-577-5170

Schaumburg
Schaumburg Schwinn
Cyclery
1228 North Roselle Road
847-882-7728

Performance Bicycle Shop
1408 Golf Road
847-240-0020

Skokie
Al's Cycle Shop
8118 Lincoln Avenue
847-673-0135

Peurye Cyclery
4049 West Main
847-676-3266

Tinley Park
Tinley Bicycle & Fitness
16906 South Oak Park
708-532-9090

Westchester
Westchester Wheels, Inc.
10411 West Cermak Road
708-562-0330

Wilmette
Wilmette Bicycle & Sport
Shop
605 Green Bay Road
847-251-1404

Winnetka
Alberto's Cycles
1075 Gage
847-446-2042

T. L. Fritts Co.
560 Chestnut Street
847-446-6694

Calendar of Events

Each event is shown under the month scheduled at time of publication. Call for more specific information.

January

Winter Festivals
Jensen Slides, Milwaukee and Devon, Chicago
Swallow Cliff, Palos Park
The Forest Preserve District of Cook County
708-771-1014 or 708-771-1062

Lake Katherine Winter Festival
Lake Katherine Nature Preserve, Palos Heights
708-361-1873

February

Nordic Ski Moonlight Outing
Deer Grove Forest Preserve, Palatine
The Forest Preserve District of Cook County
708-771-1014 or 708-771-1062

March

Golf Season Opens
(10 courses and 3 driving ranges)
The Forest Preserve District of Cook County
708-366-9420

Maple Syrup Festival
North Park Village Nature Center, Chicago
312-744-5472

Maple Syrup Festival
River Trail Nature Center, Northbrook
The Forest Preserve District of Cook County
847-824-8360

St. Patrick's Day Ride
17/35M, Wauconda
Wheeling Wheelmen
847-520-5010

Sugar Bush Fair
Spring Valley Nature Sanctuary, Schaumburg
847-985-2115

April

Bicycle Swap
Arlington Heights Bicycle Association
847-398-4633

Earth Day Events at six nature centers
The Forest Preserve District of Cook County
708-366-9420

Lake Katherine Earth Day Celebration
Lake Katherine Nature Preserve, Palos Heights
708-361-1873

Woodcock Watch
Wolf Road Prairie, Westchester
Save the Prairie Society
708-865-8736

May

Arlington 500 Invitational Bike Ride
32/45/65M (May or June)
Arlington Heights Bicycle Association
847-398-4633

Bike Ride to Fight Diabetes
11 locations throughout Chicagoland
American Diabetes Association
312-346-1805

Bike to Work Week
Chicagoland Bicycle Federation
312-42-PEDAL

Des Plaines River Canoe Marathon
Oak Spring Road, Libertyville
The Forest Preserve District of Cook County
708-771-1014 or 708-771-1062

International Migratory Bird Day
Crabtree Nature Center, Barrington
The Forest Preserve District of Cook County
847-381-6592

Tour of the North Shore
10/26/50M, Skokie
American Cancer Society
847-328-5147

Ride for Wildlife Bicycle Festival
Caldwell Woods Forest Preserve, Chicago
The Forest Preserve District of Cook County
708-771-1014 or 708-771-1062

Summer Sizzler
5K competition run and walk
Yankee Woods Forest Preserve, Oak Forest
The Forest Preserve District of Cook County
708-771-1014 or 708-771-1062

Venetian Night
Chicago Lakefront
312-744-2964

June

Boulevard Lakefront Tour
Chicago 35M bike tour
Chicagoland Bicycle Federation
312-42-PEDAL

Environmental Awareness Expo
Little Red Schoolhouse Nature Center,
Willow Springs
The Forest Preserve District of Cook County
708-839-6897

Grant Park Music Festival (June-August)
Grant Park, Chicago
312-819-0614

Jewish Folk Arts Festival
Caldwell Woods Forest Preserve, Chicago
The Forest Preserve District of Cook County
708-771-1014 or 708-771-1062

Run for the Zoo/Zoofest
Races & Kids Competitions
Lincoln Park, Chicago
312-404-2372

August

Bicycle Across the Magnificent
Miles of Illinois-BAMMI
125/500 M
American Lung Association
312-243-2000

Chicago Air & Water Show
North Avenue Beach, Chicago
312-744-3370

HeartRide
30 M tour through downtown Chicago
American Heart Association
312-346-4675

The Great Chicago to Milwaukee Bike Ride
50/100 M, Glenview
Thresholds Homeless Program
800-637-3135

Dog Daze Doubles
30/60/100/120 M bike rides
Oak Park Bicycle Club
708-482-6000

July

The L.A.T.E. Ride
25 M, after midnight starting in
Grant Park Friends of the Parks
312-918-RIDE

September

Autumn Leaves Classic
5K/10K run and 5K walk competition
Busse Woods Forest Preserve,
Rolling Meadows
The Forest Preserve District of Cook County
708-771-1014 or 708-771-1062

Harmon Hundred
17/30/60/100M Wauconda
Wheeling Wheelmen
847-520-5010

Illinois & Michigan Canal Rendezvous
Columbia Woods Forest Preserve,
Willow Springs
The Forest Preserve District of Cook County
708-771-1014
or I & M Canal National Heritage Corridor
800-926-2262

Monarch Butterfly Festival
Lake Katherine Nature Preserve,
Palos Heights
708-361-1873

North Shore Century
25/50/62/100 M Evanston
Evanston Bicycle Club
847-866-7743

Pioneer Festival
Spring Valley Nature Sanctuary, Schaumburg
847-985-2115

Prairie Appreciation Day
Wolf Road Prairie, Westchester
Save the Prairie Society
708-865-8736

Traditional Native American Pow Wow
Thatcher Woods Forest Preserve,
River Forest
The Forest Preserve District of Cook County
708-771-1014 or 708-771-1062

West Cook Bike-A-Thon
13M Salt Creek, Brookfield
American Cancer Society
708-484-8541

October

Fall Honey and Harvest Festival
River Trail Nature Center, Northbrook
The Forest Preserve District of Cook County
847-824-8360

The Halloween Haunted Forest
Caldwell Woods Forest Preserve, Chicago
The Forest Preserve District of Cook County
708-771-1014 or 708-771-1062

Harvest Festival
North Park Village Nature Center, Chicago
312-744-5472

Nature Art Fair
Little Red Schoolhouse Nature Center,
Willow Springs
The Forest Preserve District of Cook County
708-839-6897

November

Settler's Day
Sand Ridge Nature Center, South Holland
The Forest Preserve District of Cook County
708-868-0606

December

Camp Sagawau Cross-Country Ski Program,
Lemont
The Forest Preserve District of Cook County
630-257-2045

Victorian Holiday Festival
The Harold "Hal" Tyrrell Trailside Museum,
River Forest
The Forest Preserve District of Cook County
708-366-6530

The Forest Preserve District of Cook County
TDD# (hearing impaired) 708-771-1190

Organizations

Bicycle Clubs

Arlington Heights Bicycle Association
500 E. Minor Street
Arlington Heights, IL 60004
847-398-4633

Chicagoland Bicycle Federation
417 S. Dearborn, Suite 1000
Chicago, IL 60605
312-42-PEDAL

Chicago Cycling Club
P. O. Box 577136
Chicago, IL 60657
312-509-8093

Evanston Bicycle Club
P. O. Box 1981
Evanston, IL 60204
847-866-7743

League of Illinois Bicyclists
417 S. Dearborn, Suite 1000
Chicago, IL 60605
312-42-PEDAL

Mt. Prospect Bike Club
411 S. Maple
Mt. Prospect, IL 60056
847-255-5380

Oak Park Bicycle Club
P. O. Box 2331
Oak Park, IL 60303
708-482-6000

Recreation for Individuals
Dedicated to the Environment (RIDE)
Suite 1700, 208 S. LaSalle Street
Chicago, IL 60604
312-853-2820

Trail Users Rights Foundation (TURF)
P. O. Box 403
Summit, IL 60501
847-470-4266

Wheeling Wheelmen
P. O. Box 581-D
Wheeling, IL 60090
847-520-5010

Environmental

Chicago Ornithological Society
559 Clinton Place
River Forest, IL 60305
708-366-2409

Friends of the Chicago River
407 S. Dearborn Suite 1580
Chicago, IL 60605
312-939-0490

Friends of the Lake Katherine
Nature Preserve
7402 Lake Katherine Drive
Palos Heights, IL 60463
708-361-1873

Friends of the Parks
407 South Dearborn Suite 1590
Chicago, IL 60605
312-922-3307

Green Team Volunteer Program
Chicago Park District
312-747-2121

Illinois Ornithological Society
P. O. Box 1971
Evanston, IL, 60204
847-566-4846

The Nature Conservancy,
Illinois Field Office
Volunteer Stewardship Office
8 S. Michigan, Suite 900
Chicago, IL 60603
312-346-8166

Save the Prairie Society
10327 Elizabeth
Westchester, IL 60154
708-865-8736

Sierra Club-Illinois Chapter
One North LaSalle Street, Suite 4242
Chicago, IL 60612
(Includes the Chicago, Sauk-Calumet,
and Woods & Wetlands groups)
312-251-1680

Spring Valley Nature Sanctuary
Volunteer Group
1111 E. Schaumburg Road
Schaumburg, IL 60194
847-985-2115

Volunteer Stewardship Groups
Cook County Forest Preserves
12545 West 111th Street
LeMont, IL 60439
708-255-2045

Hiking and Walking

American Hiking Society
P. O. Box 20160
Washington, D. C. 20041
301-565-6704

Forest Trails Hiking Club
2025 Sherman Avenue, #407
Evanston, IL 60201
847-475-4223

Trails

The Illinois Prairie Path
P. O. Box 1086
Wheaton, IL 60189
708*-752-0120

Rails-to-Trails Conservancy
319 W. Cook Street,
Springfield, IL 62704
217-789-4782

Other

The Outings Club of Chicago
Outdoors Activities
520 N. Elizabeth
Lombard, IL 60148
708*-268-9478

*Note DuPage County's area code
changes to 630 in August 1996.

Bibliography

Books

A Short History of Chicago. Cromie, Robert. Lexikos. 1984

The Complete Guide to America's National Parks. National Park Foundation. 1992-93 Edition.

Greenways for America. Little, Charles E. Johns Hopkins University Press. 1990.

Historic Chicago Sites. Jensen, George Peter. Excella Press. 1953.

Other Publications

Designs for a Diverse Landscape: Revitalizing the Skokie Lagoons. Illinois Chapter-American Society of Landscape Architects. April 1992.

Origin and Evolution of Illinois Counties. State of Illinois. April, 1992.

State of The Greenways Report. Prepared by Northeastern Illinois Planning Commission and Openlands Project. July, 1994.

The Northeastern Illinois Regional Greenways Plan. Developed by the Northeastern Illinois Planning Commission and Openlands Project. May, 1993.

Trails for all Americans—The Report of the National Trails Agenda Project. Submitted by American Trails to the National Park Service. Summer, 1990.

About The Team

Author/publisher, Jim Hochgesang, is a hiking and biking enthusiast. Jim and his wife, Sandy, started a small self-publishing company, Roots & Wings, in spring of 1993. Since then a series of three regional hiking and biking guidebooks have been published covering Cook, DuPage, and Lake Counties. Roots & Wings guidebooks can be found in well over 200 Chicagoland stores.

Sheryl DeVore, who edited and added natural history information to all three guidebooks, has won many first place national and regional awards for her environment and nature writing. A volunteer for the Lake County Forest Preserves, Sheryl is also chief editor of *Meadowlark, A Journal of Illinois Birds*; as well as author of many nature-related articles in national magazines. She is an ardent birder and hiker.

Melanie Lawson is a designer and calligrapher living and working in the Chicago area. She is also an avid hiker.

Comments from Our Customers

Your comments related to this guidebook are very much appreciated for our use in improving future issues.

_____

_____

_____

_____

We are also considering publishing other hiking/biking guidebooks. Would you be interested in the following?

	Level of Interest		
	High	**Medium**	**Low**
• Hiking and Biking in Kane and McHenry Counties, Illinois	☐	☐	☐
• Hiking and Biking in Will and Kendall Counties, Illinois	☐	☐	☐
• Hiking and Biking in Door County, Wisconsin	☐	☐	☐
• Hiking and Biking in Southeastern Wisconsin	☐	☐	☐

We will be happy to include you on our mailing list to announce any upcoming products.

Name _____

Address _____

City, State, Zip Code _____

Thanks for your input.

Order Form

Send _____ copy/copies of First Edition Roots & Wings Hiking & Biking guidebooks to the following address:

Name _____

Address _____

City, State, Zip Code _____

Please enclose a personal check for the total amount made payable to Roots & Wings, P.O. Box 167, Lake Forest, Illinois, 60045. Thank you for your order!

_____ books @ $10.95 = _____   *Hiking & Biking in Lake County, Illinois*

_____ books @ $11.95 = _____   *Hiking & Biking in DuPage County, Illinois*

_____ books @ $12.95 = _____   *Hiking & Biking in Cook County, Illinois*

Subtotal   = _____

Illinois Residents Add
Sales Tax @ 6.5%   = _____

Shipping and Handling   = $1.95

Total   = _____

You may also buy additional copies of these guidebooks at bookstores, bicycle shops, nature stores, and outfitters as well as other merchants throughout Chicagoland.